HISPANIC WOMEN
PROPHETIC VOICE IN THE CHURCH
Toward a Hispanic Women's
Liberation Theology

MUJER HISPANA
VOZ PROFÉTICA EN LA IGLESIA
Hacia Una Teología de Liberación de la
Mujer Hispana

Ada María Isasi-Díaz
and
Yolanda Tarango, C.C.V.I.

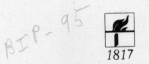

1817

Harper & Row, Publishers, San Francisco

New York, Grand Rapids, Philadelphia, St. Louis
London, Singapore, Sydney, Tokyo, Toronto

ISBN: 0-06-064095-2
Library of Congress Catalog Card Number: 87-45707

89   90   91   92   MPC   10   9   8   7   6   5   4   3

Dedicamos este libro
(We dedicate this book)

a nuestras familias
(to our families)

a las Mujeres Hispanas que luchan por vivir y por la justicia
(to Hispanic Women who struggle for survival and justice)

a Marjorie Tuite—una hermana en la lucha
(to Marjorie Tuite—a sister in the struggle)

CONTENTS

ACKNOWLEDGMENTS

We want to begin by thanking those to whom we dedicate this book. First, our families, who are usually totally prejudiced in our favor and have been an enormous source of support for us. We are most grateful to all the Hispanic Women who have shared with us their understandings and beliefs. They gave us their valuable time and insights enthusiastically; they also encouraged us to bring to fruition the theological work we had envisioned by repeatedly affirming its value. Those who have read early drafts of this book have been willing to hold us accountable.

We dedicate this book to Marjorie Tuite, OP. Her unexpected death in June of 1986 has been a great loss for us. Margie stood with Hispanic Women time and again; solidarity for her was a way of life. As one of our mentors she always affirmed and demanded even greater commitment to the grassroots people. She never stopped pushing us to analyze, to make the connections among the different oppressive structures, as well as demanding that we put our values into practice. Her legacy to us will continue always to grow because it is rooted in an *entrega*—a total self-giving to the struggle that never stops bearing fruit.

Beverly Harrison and Isabel Carter Heyward read earlier drafts of this book and offered valuable critique; together with Mary Pellauer and Rosemary Radford Ruether they were the first academic women theologians who took seriously our doing theology. They will never know how valuable their encouragement has been in our pursuing the theological task. As women theologians not belonging to the dominant culture, we appreciate their warm and persistent sisterly support.

We have to thank the feminist communities at Union Theological Seminary in New York City and at the Chicago Theological Cluster. In particular we thank: Angela Bauer, Pam Brubaker, Hyun Kyung Chung, Christina Del Piero, Cindy Derway, Katie Jeffress, Marilyn Legge, Margie Mayman-Park, Lois Kirkwood, and Serenity Young of New York; Catherine Brousseau, Brenda McCarthy, Karen McLoughlin, Rhonda Meister, Marlene Perrotte, Madalynn Smith, and Judy Vaughn of Chicago. Their support went from listening to us repeatedly to seeing that we did not get "cabin fever" during the time it took to finish this project.

We wish to thank many religious congregations, organizations, and individuals who with their financial help made this book possible. Without their contributions we never would have been able to travel to different areas of this country and meet with Hispanic Women. Among our contributors are: Center of Concern; Sisters of Charity of Cincinnati; Sisters of Charity of New York; Sisters of Charity of the Incarnate Word—San Antonio; Claretians Eastern U.S.A. Province; Dominican Sisters of Grand Rapids; Dominican Sisters of the Sick Poor; LAS HERMANAS; Little Sisters of the Assumption; Loretto Community; Sisters of Mercy—Brooklyn; Sisters of Mercy of Rochester; National Assembly of Religious Women; National Coalition of American Nuns; Presentation Sisters—Aberdeen; Sisters of the Presentation—Newburgh; Sisters of the Presentation—San Francisco; Quixote Center; Religious of the Sacred Heart—U.S. Province; Sisters of St. Anne; Sisters of St. Joseph of Peace; Sisters, Servants of the Immaculate Heart of Mary—Monroe; In Memory of Brunita and Lucio Silva; Johanna Sizick; Ursuline Sisters of Tildonk; and Leona I. Witkowski. Of course they are in no way responsible for the content of this book.

We owe a big debt of gratitude to Joyce Glover. She has been a wonderful editor, respecting Spanish thought patterns while correcting English grammar and suggesting ways of clarifying for the readers what we had not expressed adequately. Her friendly support and encouragement have been a constant source of strength. We also wish to say «muchas gracias» to Aurora Camacho de Schmidt who edited the Spanish synthesis of each chapter. Shirley Cloyes read this book when it was only a rough draft; even so, she enthusiastically endorsed it and encouraged us to finish it and submit it for publication. We thank her for all her efforts on our behalf.

Finally, we thank all those who will take seriously what we present in this book and who are willing to dialogue with us. By doing so they will be affirming what we believe: Hispanic Women are a valuable source of divine revelation and our voices must be heard, respected, and engaged.

PROLOGUE

First and foremost we are activists—Hispanic Women committed to the struggle for justice and peace. Our lived experience has pointed us in the direction of being theologians. We see no conflict in being both theologians[1] and activists; this follows our understanding of the intrinsic unity between what has been classically referred to as systematic theology and moral theology or ethics. This will become obvious as we clarify what it means for us to *do* theology.

Doing theology is a communal process. We do theology because of, for, and with other Hispanic Women with whom we participate in the struggle for liberation. Those with whom we engage in the struggle are our primary community of accountability. Therefore, the Hispanic Women's Liberation Theology we begin to elaborate in this book has to be clear to them, make sense to them, be valid for them. This is one of the reasons why we are including a synopsis of each chapter in Spanish. Hispanic Women's Liberation Theology also has to make sense to others who stand in solidarity with our struggle for liberation.

As feminists we often have been asked why we bother with religion, why we put our energies and gifts into struggling with church officials, into doing theology. We do it for several important reasons:

- A significant piece of our becoming the best possible selves we can be—which we think is what life is all about—is intrinsically

Ref.
1

?

Creencia

linked to religion. Thus we work always toward a greater understanding of what we believe, why we believe it, and how it affects
who we are/what we do.

- As Hispanics, religion—specifically Roman Catholicism—is a
very significant element of our culture. As Hispanic Women we
have been very hurt by the Catholic church in a number of
ways—and this does not refer only to hurt feelings. Many of us
even have walked away from the Catholic church and other
Christian churches. Yet, as a group of us told a U.S. Bishops'
Committee, "We cannot leave the Church. It is part of our
culture, of who we are!"

- For Hispanics the church has provided not only our religious
frameworks but also the main paradigms for our "moods and
motivations"[2] in life.

- As Hispanic feminists struggling for liberation, we believe the
church plays a powerful role in our oppression. The church
sanctions—justifies—the patriarchy in society by being itself a
patriarchal structure. If the church is holy and patriarchal, is
not patriarchy holy? If the church were to denounce patriarchy,
it would be an important moment in the process of the liberation
of women. For this reason, as Roman Catholics, we must continue to call the Catholic church to repent of the sexism inherent
in its structures and in some of its tenets.

Throughout this book we will be using the phrase "Hispanic
Women's Liberation Theology." There are difficulties in using the
term *Hispanic* to name ourselves because it is the way the dominant
structures of the United States refer to us. Most of us call ourselves
according to the country of our ethnic roots. Others prefer to be called
Latinas. However, we have chosen to use the term *Hispanic* in this
book because it is the one commonly used in this society.

When we say "Hispanic Women," we do not have a sense of
representing Hispanic Women at large. Hispanic Women are too
many, too different, to be spoken for by a couple of us. Rather, we
speak *as* Hispanic Women who struggle for liberation. However, we,

the authors of this book, do not believe that our voices are solitary or that they are much different from those of other Hispanic Women. Much of what we say here of our own theological understandings we have heard repeatedly. It is what other Hispanic Women have told us. We have spoken intentionally about our views of theology with many Hispanic Women and have listened carefully to their comments, agreements, and disagreements. We have given the material in this book to Hispanic Women to critique and evaluate. They have assured us that the work truly reflects their religious beliefs and practices.

In the United States Hispanics include the vast numbers of Mexican Americans whose home for many generations has been the southwestern part of this country. As we love to point out, the fact that this area was not always part of the United States indicates that the border crossed us—we did not cross the border. Hispanics are also people who come from and/or whose historical-cultural roots are in Mexico, Central and South America, and the Caribbean—countries having Spanish as the common language of the people. That we now make our home in the United States does not necessarily mean that we are never going to return to our countries of origin. It simply means that, for whatever reason, we have had to or have freely decided to live here while clearly claiming a cultural legacy different from that of indigenous North Americans, North Americans of African descent, of Anglo-Saxon descent, and of other European descent.

In this book Hispanics refer to people who are aware and critically conscious of the place and role we have in this society because of who we are culturally. The three main groups we have in mind when we use the term Hispanic in this book are Mexican Americans, Puerto Ricans, and Cubans. Hispanic refers to the coming together here in the United States of these three groups with their cultural variants. This coming together necessarily brings about cultural modifications and innovations which, over a period of time, become a new culture.

But the main characters in this book are not the Hispanic people but Hispanic *Women*. Hispanic Women's culture differs from Hispanic men's culture in certain specific ways. This is due mainly to the sexism that is part of both the Hispanic culture and the dominant

Anglo culture. Our socialization as women—what society expects of us as women and the limitations imposed on us because we are women—contributes to the distinctive features of Hispanic Women's culture. These distinctive features are also the result of the coming together of classism/economic oppression and sexism, and of ethnic prejudice and sexism. This coming together of oppressions does not mean that we suffer two, or at times three, different kinds of oppression. It is rather a compounding into one multilayered oppression.[3] Our claim as Hispanic Women is not that we are unique but that we are distinct. Our claim is that some of the reasons for our oppression do not apply to Hispanic men and to other oppressed groups.

"Hispanic Women's Liberation Theology" means two things in this book. First, as the sub-title of the book indicates, it means *"toward a* Hispanic Women's Liberation Theology." This book simply begins to identify the theological understandings, motivations, and actions of Hispanic Women. Second, Hispanic Women's Liberation Theology brings together feminist theology, cultural theology, and liberation theology.

- It is cultural theology because "theology is the product of culture."[4] It is cultural theology because, as "residents in an alien land," our religious understandings are intrinsic to our struggle against assimilation. We struggle to maintain the values of our culture as an intrinsic element of our self-identity and of our struggle. Being Hispanic is not a choice, but what we do with our Hispanic-ness is a choice we make again and again.
- It is feminist theology because we know that the oppression of women by men is an intrinsic element of all oppression. The struggle against sexism and its incarnational mode, patriarchy, is a significant element of our doing theology.
- It is liberation theology because we do not seek to participate in oppressive structures but to change those structures; our goal is not equality but liberation. The socio-political-economic oppression we suffer, which places Hispanic Women at the

bottom of the economic ladder in this country, is at the heart of our theology.

These three perspectives intertwine to form a whole; they critique and challenge each other, they inform each other. Hispanic Women's Liberation Theology is more than the sum of its parts; it is a synthesis that gives birth to new elements, to a new reality.

The cultural or Hispanic perspective contributes to Hispanic Women's Liberation Theology the claim that Hispanic culture is valuable and has significant contributions to make (other than its music, food, and dress!) to what is normative in this society, in the church. Hispanic Women's Liberation Theology emphasizes the importance of the African and Amerindian strands in the culture. It insists especially on the important role these two strands play in the religiosity of the people. This insistence critiques the racism/ethnic prejudice to which feminism in the United States and Latin American Liberation Theology seem to be prone. Both have failed to take into consideration the experiences and understandings of racial/ethnic persons. At best, feminism in the United States and Latin American Liberation Theology have attempted to adapt and incorporate into their movements the racial/ethnic understandings that *they* consider important. However, neither of them have been willing to accept the contributions of racial/ethnic persons as intrinsic elements of their theologies.

The feminist perspective brings to Hispanic Women's Liberation Theology the insistence on personal experience as the starting point in the process of liberation and, therefore, in the doing of theology. It also makes significant contributions to methodology by its rejection of the dualism and hierarchical principles that underlie the classical approach to theology.[5] Both are constructs of patriarchy and, in rejecting them, feminism critiques the sexism in both Latin American and other Third World Liberation Theologies as well as the sexism in Hispanic culture. Third World Liberation Theologies have largely ignored and/or refused to deal with the oppression of women.

The Hispanic culture, like all cultures but no more than any other culture, considers and treats women as inferior to men.

The liberation perspective brings to Hispanic Women's Liberation Theology the understandings of liberation and conscientization and an insistence on the socio-political-economic aspect of all oppression. It critiques the elitism often present in feminism and denounces the tendency of Hispanics to lose themselves in the Anglo world, to buy into the dominant culture, to seek an individualistic way out of oppression.

A question raised time and again by the approach used in this book as well as by the understandings presented is that of authority. The source of Hispanic Women's Liberation Theology is Hispanic Women's experience, and both Scripture and Christian tradition are dealt with insofar as they inform and are part of Hispanic Women's experience and contribute to their liberation. Given these approaches, what is authoritative is the experience of the Hispanic Women's community. What does this mean?

- The sense of security that authority has given us all is found not in following what others say, but in struggling to be self-defining.
- The comfortable certainty that sameness provides is relinquished in favor of the certainty provided by the dimension of struggle in our lives.
- Right and wrong are evaluated/defined in terms of the common good; that is why orthopraxis and not orthodoxy is key. The common good of Hispanic Women cannot be defined apart from the common good of other communities of struggle.
- Scripture and Christian tradition are not rejected but rather seen through the lens of Hispanic Women's experience. What is rejected is the patriarchal institutional lens of the church as the only or most important normative lens.

The process by which we have arrived at the formulations presented here is anything but linear. We have proceeded in an inductive way, moving from our experience and the experience that other

Hispanic Women have shared with us, to systematic reflection, and finally coming to suggest theological formulations. As academically trained theologians, we have also used a deductive method: we have derived and grasped theological insights and understandings from our readings of other theologies that we have then "checked out" against our experience and the experience of other Hispanic Women. Some of these theological insights have been incorporated into Hispanic Women's Liberation Theology; others have been modified; others have been totally rejected.

But the question of whether our methodology is inductive or deductive is not of great concern to us. What we are concerned about is how to present our experience and the experience of other Hispanic Women in a nonmanipulative way, in an honest way. After long thought and extensive consultation, we have decided that the only honest way to deal with the material gathered in our meetings with Hispanic Women is first to present a representative selection of their words verbatim. This procedure most honestly expresses the main goal of this book, which is to provide an opportunity for the voices of Hispanic Women to be heard. We are not trying to mystify Hispanic Women's voices. We are simply asserting that our voices are an intrinsic part of the human voice and therefore should be an intrinsic part of all theology.

Hispanic Women's experiences and how they understand those experiences are at the core of Hispanic Women's Liberation Theology. That is why Hispanic Women's voices, their very own words, are at the heart of this book. Therefore, we have purposefully dedicated at least half of this book to recording their words verbatim. The rest—the analytical chapters—are complementary, suggestive, and understandable only in view of the verbatim material.

We realize that the verbatim material in this book already is an interpretation. First of all, it was originally spoken mostly in Spanish and in Spanglish, a combination of Spanish and English not only within a given phrase but even within given words. What we present here is a translation, and we know that all translation is interpretation. Second, we chose to present a few Hispanic Women's voices from among many. We chose as much of a variety as possible: Mexican American, Puerto Rican, Cuban voices; voices from different socioeconomic strata and with different degrees of schooling; voices of older and younger women; voices of women who are involved in church movements as well as voices of women for whom church is peripheral; voices with which we agree and voices with which we disagree. But, undoubtedly, regardless of our attempts to be as inclusive as possible, our choosing is colored by our own understandings, perspectives, and faith tradition—and that is interpretation. One last mode of interpretation we could not avoid has to do with editing. Though it has been minimal and done with the intention of clarifying instead of controlling the material, any and all editing is interpretative.

Besides presenting some of the voices of Hispanic Women, in the verbatim chapters we also begin to point out a few of the central words and ideas found in the material gathered and to analyze them so as to understand what Hispanic Women are saying regarding certain "traditional theological themes" such as salvation, sin, grace, and God. This task of organizing and analyzing the material is presented here in an abbreviated form. The criterion for this decision is our belief that the most important thing is what Hispanic Women think and say and not an interpretation of it. Our reflection upon Hispanic Women's experience, including our own, is intrinsic to the doing of theology. Extensive reflection and some systematization will perhaps be our task in a second book. However, in this book, the analysis included is intended mainly to present all aspects of the process we are following in the formulation of Hispanic Women's Liberation Theology rather than to delineate and systematize theological understandings.

We do not pretend to be, nor would we want to be, objective in our theological pursuit. We do not believe objectivity is a value; we question its feasibility. Because we believe that nothing escapes historical conditioning, subjectivity is a day-to-day reality. What honesty demands of us, what the limitedness of our subjectivity requires, is for us to identify our subjectivity and then balance that subjectivity with that of others involved in the community of struggle.[6] Objectivity for us means "openness to others' history and to the critical claims that history bears and also the ability to learn from others' historical experience." The only objectivity we seek "is the one of an engagement, a militancy." It is our hope that Hispanic Women's Liberation Theology will always be a "passionate language" because our survival is indeed at stake.[7]

Finally, we want to identify some of the basic presuppositions that ground our lives and, therefore, our praxis. These presuppositions will help explain some of what is being said in this book.

- When in doubt, we act, for if we do not, possibilities will never unfold.
- Risk is part of life, so we do not try to avoid it. We may be afraid, but not paralyzed.
- Divine revelation is always happening in the community and through the community.
- Our goal, our hope, is the creation of the community of struggle: that is what the "kin-dom"[8] of God is all about. The common good of the community is one of our main preoccupations, a common good that cannot fall under ideological control and is always being understood anew.
- Leadership belongs to the community, and to hold accountable those whom the community appoints to exercise it is both the right and obligation of the community. As "theological technicians" we, the authors of this book, offer leadership to the doing of theology in which the community engages.
- Joy is an intrinsic part of the work for justice and peace. Joy is an expression of hope, which gives a most important spark to our struggle. As a joyful community we express our belief in the presence of the divine among us and in us, a presence that pushes us on because, in our being fulfilled, divinity is fully revealed.

Síntesis del Prólogo

Ante todo somos activistas—Mujeres Hispanas comprometidas con la lucha por la justicia y la paz. Parte intrínseca de nuestra lucha es el «hacer teología»—un proceso de la comunidad y en favor de la comunidad. Por lo tanto es a la comunidad de Mujeres Hispanas a la que rendimos cuentas de lo que aquí escribimos. Sólo en segunda instancia rendimos cuenta a la comunidad de teólogos académicos.

Sabemos que la expresión *Hispanas* no es necesariamente la más indicada para describirnos. La mayoría de nosotras nunca usamos la palabra sino que nos identificamos según el país de nuestras raíces étnicas—mexicano-americanas, puertorriqueñas, cubanas. Si usamos *Hispanas* en este libro es simplemente porque es el término que más se usa en esta sociedad.

Al hablar acerca de las Mujeres Hispanas no hablamos como si las representáramos. Hablamos *como* Mujeres Hispanas convencidas de que nuestra manera de pensar y nuestras razones no son diferentes a las de otras Mujeres Hispanas. Durante más de diez años hemos compartido nuestro sentido religioso con otras Mujeres Hispanas en diferentes partes de este país. Varias Mujeres Hispanas han leído este libro y nos han asegurado que lo que aquí decimos refleja lo que ellas creen y viven.

¿Quiénes son las Mujeres Hispanas a las que nos referimos? Son las mujeres mexicano-americanas que por muchas generaciones han vivido en el suroeste de los Estados Unidos. Son también las mujeres cuyas raíces históricas y culturales se encuentran en México y el Caribe. El que mexicanas, puertorriqueñas, y cubanas ahora vivamos en Estados Unidos no quiere decir que nunca regresaremos a nuestra tierra natal. Simplemente quiere decir que por muchas razones diferentes tuvimos que venir a vivir en este país o simplemente decidimos hacerlo. Pero eso no quiere decir que no reclamemos una herencia cultural diferente a la de los indígenas norteamericanos, norteamericanos de descendencia africana, de descendencia anglo-sajona u otras culturas europeas. En este texto se usa el término *Mujeres Hispanas* para designar a las mujeres cubanas, mexicano-americanas, y puertorriqueñas que estamos concientes de la opresión que sufrimos en esta sociedad precisamente por ser Mujeres Hispanas. Consideramos que algunas de las razones por las cuales sufrimos opresión son distintas a las razones por las cuales tanto los hombres Hispanos como hombres y mujeres de otros grupos raciales y étnicos sufren opresión.

Lo que pretendemos con este libro es comenzar un diálogo. Es por eso que los lectores no deben olvidar dos palabras muy importantes del sub-título del libro: *Hacia* y *una*. No pretendemos, ni presentar una obra terminada, ni que los entendimientos teológicos que se presentan en este libro sean los únicos de las Mujeres Hispanas. Esta teología de la liberación de la Mujer Hispana trata simplemente de identificar algunas formulaciones teológicas, y las motivaciones y acciones religiosas de Mujeres Hispanas. Esta teología conjuga elementos que están presentes en las teologías feministas con elementos de teología cultural y teología de la liberación. La interacción entre estos elementos genera una síntesis de la que nacen nuevos elementos—una nueva realidad.

En este libro no pretendemos ser objetivas. Lo que queremos es identificar nuestra perspectiva, establecer la importancia que tiene, y estar abiertas a las perspectivas de todos los grupos que luchan por la liberación.

Por último, queremos identificar las presuposiciones que son parte tanto de nuestras vidas como de nuestra teología.

- Las dudas no nos paralizan; preferimos actuar aún cuando tenemos dudas porque sino algunas ideas, posiblemente muy valiosas, nunca se convertirán en realidad.
- El riesgo es parte de la vida así que no tratamos de evitarlo. A veces tenemos miedo pero no dejamos que nos paralice.
- La revelación divina ocurre continuamente. Siempre está ocurriendo en la comunidad y a través de la comunidad.
- Nuestra meta, nuestra esperanza, es crear la comunidad de lucha: el florecimiento del pueblo de Dios. Lo que nos preocupa es el bien de la comunidad—una comunidad que lucha en contra

de todo control ideológico y que siempre trata de entenderse «de nuevo».

- El liderazgo de la comunidad es parte intrínseca de la misma. La comunidad a la vez pide y concede a algunas de sus miembros el ejercer ese liderazgo de acuerdo con los dones de las personas y las necesidades de la comunidad. Las autoras de este libro somos «técnicas teológicas»—líderes en el proceso teológico de la comunidad.

- La alegría es parte intrínseca del trabajo en favor de la justicia y la paz. La alegría es expresión de nuestra esperanza, de nuestra lucha. Como comunidad alegre, expresamos nuestra creencia en la presencia divina entre nosotras y en nosotras que nos hace seguir luchando porque sabemos que nuestra liberación hará posible ver claramente la revelación divina.

Chapter 1

HISPANIC WOMEN'S LIBERATION THEOLOGY: BEGINNINGS

Hispanic Women's Liberation Theology is a praxis—critical, reflective action based on and dealing with questions of ultimate meaning. This praxis is a reflective action based on analysis of a historical reality done through the lens of an option for and a commitment to liberation of Hispanic Women. A clear understanding of the use of the word *praxis* is very important.

Praxis is not reflection that follows action or is "at the service of action."[1] Both action and reflection become inseparable moments in praxis.

Praxis "combines reflection with action to create the human world of ideas, symbols, language, science, religion, art, and production." To bring reflection to bear upon action—that is praxis.[2]

Truth is relevant at the level of action, "not in the realm of ideas." Therefore, like other liberation theologies, Hispanic Women's Liberation Theology is concerned not with orthodoxy but with orthopraxis.[3]

Soteriology, the study of the doctrine of salvation, has always been an intrinsic part of theology. Hispanic Women's Liberation Theology as praxis incarnates soteriology; it takes seriously the integration of the human and the divine, not only in the person of Jesus but also in the history of all human beings and the role this integration plays in the doctrine of salvation. By bringing together soteriology and praxis, Hispanic Women's Liberation Theology appropriates the sense of salvation history prevalent in the Hebrew Scriptures and in the Gospel teachings. Hispanic Women's Liberation Theology is a praxis precisely because Matthew 24:34ff. is an imperative for all those who call themselves Christians. "What you did to these, the least of my sisters and brothers, you did to me" is one of the Scripture passages that clearly indicates that soteriology has to be deeply concerned with this world's events, with tangible, day-to-day experiences—with praxis.

Because Hispanic Women's Liberation Theology is praxis, it demands three very clear and concrete commitments: to *do* theology; to do theology from a *specific* perspective; to do theology from a specific perspective *as a communal process*.

To *do* theology is to free theology from the exclusive hold of academia; it is also a matter of denouncing the false dichotomy between thought and action so prevalent in Western culture. To do theology is to recognize that the source of theology is human existence, its questions and concerns as well as its beliefs. To do theology is to validate and uphold the lived experience of the oppressed, since the dominant cultures and countries not only deny its validity, but even question its very existence.

"Theology as sure knowledge, or *scientia*, is probably the most common form of theology in Roman Catholicism and mainline Protestantism in the West today."[4] In contrast, the understanding of theology as praxis is quite common in oppressed societies throughout the world; it is a given in all liberation theologies. Hispanic Women's Liberation Theology espouses the doing of theology because it recognizes that what motivates and urges on Hispanic Women in their struggle for survival—in their struggle to become as fully human as God intends them to be, in their struggle for "salvation"—comes precisely from their religious understandings and practices.[5]

To do theology from a *specific perspective* requires a clear identification of the day-to-day life of those engaged in doing this theology, their needs and their struggles. Because of this, it is presumptuous to speak of "theology" as if there were only one and as if theology were an objective science. Likewise, it is unacceptable to speak of

Theology (with a capital T) as if there were only one true way to deal with questions of ultimate meaning. "theology" or "Theology" is, therefore, acceptable only as a heuristic device that provides a "space" in which the different theologies can meet to discuss their commonalities and differences in order to deepen their understandings. This conversation is an important one for the different theologies to engage in because the struggles to which they relate are interconnected.

Hispanic Women's Liberation Theology as a praxis has as its base and lens an option, a commitment. It does not try to be objective but rather to state clearly its subjectivity at the levels of analysis and strategy. Because of this, the particularities out of which Hispanic Women's Liberation Theology emerges become important:

1. Due to the sexism and ethnic prejudice they suffer, Hispanic Women face a most perilous situation. Classism, especially the economics of classism, is part of the oppression of the majority of Hispanic Women.
2. There is a lack of recognition by Hispanic men of Hispanic Women and their oppression.
3. Hispanic Women have come to understand that they have a very important contribution to make. The particularity of their oppression has led them to understand that the solution to their oppression has to be liberation and not equality.

Concretely, this last point means that Hispanic Women do not seek greater participation within the present oppressive patriarchal structures of both church and society. Because these structures are patriarchal, they are based on dualistic and hierarchical understandings. Thus, by their very nature they will oppress someone. Out of the particularity of their situation Hispanic Women have come to understand that a radical change in these structures is the only possible solution to oppression. Though differing in ways of doing it, they seek a shift in paradigm; it is not a matter of changing positions with males and with Anglos or sharing equally with them. It is a matter of bringing about a new reality; Hispanic Women believe that they have a distinct and valuable contribution to make to such a task.

Out of these particularities arise the questions of ultimate meaning with which Hispanic Women's Liberation Theology is preoccupied: questions of survival. Survival has to do with more than barely living. Survival has to do with the struggle *to be* fully. To survive, one has to have "the power to decide about one's history and one's vocation or historical mission."[6] This translates into two sets of questions: questions about physical survival and questions about cultural-historical survival. Though these two aspects of survival are closely linked in many given situations, they are not identical. To keep these two different aspects of survival in mind is especially important for theologies of "remnant groups"[7]—groups excluded from participation in setting the norm and distributing the resources—in First World countries. In comparison with the reality of so-called Third World countries, physical survival is not a constant preoccupation for these remnant groups, though it is not by any means far removed. The questions of ultimate meaning that Hispanic Women's Liberation Theology engages have to do not only with the survival of Hispanic Women but also with the survival of their children, their families.

These questions also are questions of ultimate meaning simply because they are voiced by Hispanic Women who are made in the image of God.

Christian theology for centuries refused to attribute the fullness of the *imago dei* to women. . . . Men were thought to participate in the *imago dei* primarily and fully, while women participated in it secondarily and partially. . . .

Not only could women not represent God to the Christian community, they could not represent the generically human—before God or before the community.[8]

Given this distorted understanding about women operating even today, to declare that questions formulated by women are questions of ultimate meaning constitutes in itself a most important theological statement. When these women are women belonging to a "remnant" group considered to be intellectually inferior because of their lack of accomplishments in the field of academia and the published word, then claiming that the questions of Hispanic Women are questions of ultimate meaning becomes a threat to the dominant groups and a strategy for Hispanic Women.

Hispanic Women's Liberation Theology rejects the idea that women are not made in the image of God. Hispanic Women as oppressed women are indeed *imago dei* insofar as they struggle to become fully human. Hispanic Women can and do image God because they are engaged in the lifelong process of becoming fully human. To be fully human does not depend on gender, race, or class, but on the willingness to be in relationship. Relationship requires commitment to vulnerability, justice, truth—love. No relationship is private, for all relationships contribute to the building up of the community. It is in this sense that the personal is political.[9]

The specificity of Hispanic Women's Liberation Theology has cultural-historical reality as its *locus theologicus*. This immediately places the theological task in contact with three very different cultures and histories: the Amerindian, the African, and the Spanish. Not all of these cultures are equally present in the different Hispanic Women's groups. Hispanic Women with ethnic roots in the Mexican culture are mostly influenced by Amerindian and Spanish culture. Hispanic Women with ethnic roots in the Caribbean, both Puerto Ricans and Cubans, are mostly influenced by African and Spanish culture. However, some small strands of all three cultures appear in all three groups.

La Raza, the race, is the *mestizaje* that has resulted from the mixture of these three races, cultures, and histories.[10] Hispanics are *mestizos* belonging indeed to *la raza*. Therefore, the Hispanic understandings of the divine, the human, the meaning of life—these understandings emerge from this *mestizaje*. The theological task of any and every Hispanic cannot ignore this three-pronged *mestizaje*. Though the Hispanic cultural-historical reality is often ignored in theology, the present and active popular religiosity of the Hispanic community requires that theology give equal consideration to all three cultural strata out of which this *mestizaje* emerges. Up to now almost exclusive attention has been given to the Catholicism brought by the Spaniards. But in popular religiosity the religious, cosmological, theological, and anthropological understandings that the Amerindians and the Africans brought to America are just as operative.

Besides culture and popular religiosity, Hispanic Women's Liberation Theology has to take into consideration the social sciences so as to include in its perspective an economic-political analysis and to avoid falling into a romantic attitude regarding culture.[11] Because of the different economic-political statuses of different groups of Hispanic Women in the United States (see Chapter 3), this could prove increasingly to be one of the most difficult variants with which Hispanic Women's Liberation Theology has to deal. Does culture prevail over economics and politics? Or are political ideology and economics more relevant or determining than culture when it comes to questions of ultimate meaning, when it comes to religious understandings and practices?

Hispanic Women's Liberation Theology is a *communal process*. There are three main reasons for this. First, the source of Hispanic Women's Liberation Theology is the lived experience, experience that has to include both personal and communal aspects. "Personal experience borders on solipsism if it is not mediated by community experience. Likewise the community's experience tends toward abstraction if it is not mediated by individual experiences."[12]

Second, the theological process is an intrinsic part of the liberation task because it is one of the ways in which the community becomes the agent of its own history. Liberation is a personal process that takes place within a community and through a community. Liberation is at the very core "the unfolding of all of man's [sic] dimensions," and, therefore, has to do not only with an "interior liberation" but also with "liberation from exterior pressures which prevent his [sic] fulfillment as a member of a certain social class, country, or society."[13] Therefore, the link between liberation and theology points to the need for theology to be a communal undertaking.

Third, one of the most pervasive themes in Hispanic culture is the community. *La comunidad* is the immediate reality within which

Hispanics find their personal identities and function. In concrete terms, the sense of community revolves around the *familia* (family) and the *barrio, barriada* (neighborhood).[14] Certain aspects of the *iglesia* (church) also provide an important focus for the development and maintenance of the sense of community among Hispanics. Social functions, such as fairs and other fundraising activities, as well as processions, novenas, and other religious functions that are a part of popular religiosity, are the aspects of church that relate to the sense of community. Though these sorts of church functions attract mostly the older people, particularly the women, they are so much part of the community that the young people will relate to them as they grow older.

Another reason why the sense of community is so important for Hispanics is their need to be a distinct group since they do not belong to the dominant culture. As a culture within another culture, Hispanics need to establish a clear sense of "us" distinguishable from Anglos, blacks, and all other ethnic/cultural groups in the United States.[15] For all these reasons, the importance of *la comunidad*, communal understandings and practices, should not be bypassed or suspended when it comes to theology.

To say that Hispanic Women's Liberation Theology is a praxis is to claim that it is organic theology (see Chapter 5). To understand theology as organic is to claim unequivocally that Hispanic Women have always acted and that their action has had a reflective quality. Have Hispanic Women, without thinking, done only what is expected of them, what Hispanic men have told them to do? Have they simply followed directions? The traditional "submission" and "passivity" that have been ascribed to Hispanic Women are not necessarily to be understood as inability to think and act or as weakness and lack of courage. Are not "submissiveness" and "passivity" strategies for survival? It is not that Hispanic Women have not engaged in praxis; the problem is that Hispanic Women's praxis has not been understood and, therefore, has not been valued.

Hispanic Women's Liberation Theology is organic theology insofar as it is "vitally engaged in historical realities with specific times and places." It is organic because it "arises spontaneously and inevitably in the believer. . . . "[16] It is organic because it engages the whole person and does not need to use sophisticated academic tools that are not available to most Hispanic Women. The essential element called for in doing Hispanic Women's Theology is to believe in one's intrinsic value as a human being, to be willing to share openly, and to ask questions seriously.

Hispanic Women's Liberation Theology is organic theology because it simply voices certain specific aspects of the day-to-day, of the "natural" activity of Hispanic Women. Hispanic Women's Liberation Theology intends to work out and make coherent "the principles and the problems raised by . . . [Hispanic Women] in their practical activity,"[17] thus becoming part of the cultural and social aspects of their culture. As organic theology, Hispanic Women's Liberation Theology both starts with the praxis—"practical activity"—of Hispanic Women and is the praxis of Hispanic Women. Praxis is intellectual enterprise as well as action. The dichotomy between intellectual activity and action that involves physical work is a fictitious one. Because Hispanic Women's Liberation Theology is organic theology, this kind of fictitious dichotomy is strictly avoided.

When one distinguishes between intellectuals and non-intellectuals, one is referring in reality only to the immediate social function of the professional category of the intellectuals, that is, one has in mind the direction in which their specific professional activity is weighted, whether towards intellectual elaboration or towards muscular-nervous effort. This means that, although one can speak of intellectuals, one cannot speak of non-intellectuals, because non-intellectuals do not exist. But even the relationship between efforts of intellectual-cerebral elaboration and muscular-nervous efforts is not always the same, so that there are varying degrees of specific intellectual activity. There is no human activity from which every form of intellectual participation can be excluded: *homo faber* cannot be separated from *homo sapiens.* Each man [*sic*], finally, outside his [*sic*] professional activity, carries on some form of intellectual activity, that is, he [*sic*] is "philosopher," an artist, a man [*sic*] of taste, he [*sic*] participates in a particular conception of the world, has a conscious line of moral conduct, and therefore contributes to sustain a conception of the world or to modify it, that is, to bring into being new modes of thought.[18]

One of the struggles of Hispanic Women's Liberation Theology is to elaborate the intellectual activity of Hispanic Women and ensure that "the muscular-nervous effort itself, in so far as it is an element of a general practical activity [praxis], which is perpetually innovating the physical and social world, becomes the foundation of a new and integral conception of the world,"[19] and, therefore, of theology.

Apuntes para una teología de la liberación de la Mujer Hispana

La teología de la liberación de la Mujer Hispana que aquí se presenta es una práxis, es decir, una acción reflexiva, crítica, que trata temas de significado fundamental y se basa en ellos. La práxis es acción reflexiva basada en el análisis de una realidad histórica, análisis que usa como lente la opción por la liberación de la Mujer Hispana y el compromiso con esa opción. Este compromiso es triple. Es un comprometerse: a *hacer* teología; a hacer teología desde una perspectiva *específica*; a hacer teología desde una perspectiva específica usando un *proceso comunitario*.

El *hacer* teología libera la teología de las manos de los teólogos académicos y niega la falsa separación entre acción y reflexión. El hacer teología desde una perspectiva *específica* quiere decir que la realidad que viven las Mujeres Hispanas es importante. Esta realidad es una situación muy peligrosa debido al sexismo y al prejuicio étnico que ellas sufren. El clasismo, y en especial su aspecto económico, es parte de la opresión que sufren las Mujeres Hispanas. Esta realidad opresiva no es reconocida por los hombres Hispanos. Pero así y todo las Mujeres Hispanas saben que tienen una contribución muy importante que hacer. Las Mujeres Hispanas no quieren igualdad con los hombres dentro de las estructuras opresivas de la iglesia y la sociedad. Ellas saben que la verdadera liberación depende de un cambio radical de las estructuras patriarcales que controlan al mundo entero.

La liberación de la Mujer Hispana tiene que ver con la supervivencia. Sobrevivir quiere decir poder desarrollarse plenamente como ser humano. Para poder sobrevivir uno tiene que poder decidir por sí misma—ser sujeto de su propia historia. La supervivencia, por lo tanto, es cultural e histórica al igual que física. Y no se trata sólo de la supervivencia de la Mujer Hispana, sino también de la supervivencia de sus hijas e hijos—de sus familias.

La supervivencia de la Mujer Hispana es una cuestión fundamental porque ella está hecha a imagen y semejanza de Dios. Esto en sí tiene gran importancia teológica: la lucha de la Mujer Hispana es una cuestión teológica ya que hace posible conocer y entender quién y cómo es Dios. También hace explicita la creencia que el ser plenamente humano, participar de lo divino, no depende del sexo de la persona, ni de su etnicidad o raza, ni de su clase social. El ser plenamente humana depende de la capacidad y el deseo de relacionarse con los demás. Esto requiere ser vulnerable, luchar por ser justo—amar. Ninguna relación es privada, ya que todo relación contribuye a edificar la comunidad. Es por eso que lo personal siempre es político.

Debido a que la teología se desarrolla en medio de la realidad cultural e histórica de la Mujer Hispana, esta teología de la liberación de la Mujer Hispana tiene que tomar en cuenta tanto la historia y la cultura española como la africana y la amerindia. Las tres son parte de la realidad de la Mujer Hispana y tienen un papel definitivo e importante en su religión. Es en la religiosidad popular donde mayormente se encuentran elementos de estas tres culturas.

Por último, esta teología de la liberación de la Mujer Hispana es un *proceso comunitario*. Hay tres razones que subrayan este hecho. Primero, la fuente principal de esta teología de la liberación de la Mujer Hispana es la experiencia de las Mujeres Hispanas —experiencia personal y comunitaria. Segundo, el proceso teológico es parte integral del proceso de liberación—un proceso personal que se desarrolla en medio de la comunidad y a través de ella. Tercero, la comunidad es un elemento muy importante en la cultura Hispana—elemento que se vuelve aún más importante toda vez que la cultura Hispana es una cultura minoritaria en este país.

Esta teología de la liberación de la Mujer Hispana es una praxis, por lo cual es también orgánica. Esto implica que las acciones de las Mujeres Hispanas son acciones concientes, y que esta teología está comprometida con estas acciones—realidades que se desarrollan en un lugar y en un período histórico específicos. Esta teología de la liberación de la Mujer Hispana es una teología orgánica porque simplemente da a conocer algunos aspectos específicos de lo que es la actividad natural diaria de las Mujeres Hispanas.

Chapter 2

IN THEIR OWN WORDS, HISPANIC WOMEN'S UNDERSTANDINGS OF THE DIVINE

The material that follows was gathered at meetings of different groups of Hispanic Women. Brief details about each one of the women quoted precedes what each of them said. Some of the names given to the women in this book are their own; others are not.

The groups were brought together in different ways by the two authors of this book. They knew some of the women who participated and arranged for them to meet. Others came because they knew and trusted the person whom the authors had asked to gather the group. At times the women in a given group knew each other previous to this meeting, but that was not always so.

The first group helped the authors to finish designing the process used. It was the first group that gave the weekend the title of "retreat"—they felt that it had been a time of personal reflection and that it had helped them very much. The women were told beforehand, and it was explained to them at length once all were together, that what they were saying would be used for a book on Hispanic Women's Liberation Theology. They were informed that the material would be used in such a way as to insure their anonymity. It was explained to them how monies for the project were gathered mainly through contributions from canonical congregations of women religious.

The women did not pay for the expenses of the weekend. Furthermore, at the end of the weekend they were given a small stipend or a gift for their participation. Only the women in one of the groups knew beforehand that they were going to receive money for participating. Most of the women initially did not want to accept the money. However, after it was explained to them that grassroots people were often used/studied by others without receiving compensation for the contributions they made, that their contribution was extremely valuable, and that women need to stop operating out of a "volunteer mentality," all of them but one accepted the money or gift.

For the most part, the group dynamics were quite smooth. The women encouraged each other, questioned each other, listened carefully to what each one had to say. The task of the authors acting as enablers was minimal, only that of announcing the topics around which discussion centered and then of participating in the discussion. The topics were always presented in question form, and the women spoke freely. The women were anxious to talk and needed little or no encouragement to do so. As a matter of fact, it was at times necessary to ask different ones to abbreviate their sharing. In only one of the groups the dynamics were quite difficult due to extraneous factors. Facilitating this one weekend process proved very tedious. The weekend turned out to be a prolonged question-and-answer period instead of a quite smooth, free-flowing conversation as it was with the rest of the groups.

Most of the time, the conversations followed a stream-of-consciousness pattern. Some of the women answered in what may be considered a nondirect or nonconcrete way. Maybe that is because they had not thought much about some of the questions they were asked. However, what might commonly be considered "style" instead clearly denotes differences in the way Hispanic Women conceptualize and express themselves. This became obvious, not only when the women talked in Spanish, but even when they spoke in English. The translation and/or editing presented here seeks to respect Hispanic Women's thought patterns.

The weekends started with each of the women taking quite a long time to tell the group about her life and whether or not she was satisfied with it. Then the group started to explore their sense of God, their idea of God. How was that sense formed? Who taught them to pray? What were the first prayers they learned? As they were growing up, did the adults in their house pray, go to church, talk about God? To whom do they pray in the most difficult moments? How would they describe God? How do they relate to Jesus Christ? The answer of each woman to all of these questions was not given all at once since each one took turns addressing the different questions suggested to help focus their thinking.

Inez

Inez, a Puerto Rican woman, was known by all of the other participants in the group. As a matter of fact, she helped the enablers pull the group together. She was a friend of everyone there, even those who knew no one else. Inez was born in the United States but was raised by her grandparents in a rural setting in Puerto Rico. She is an *independentista*—never giving up hope that one day Puerto Rico will be independent. After finishing high school in the early 1970s, she entered the convent. She was sent to another Latin American country to do her novitiate. There she spent three difficult and painful years and, in the end, was not allowed to make vows. After that she moved to the United States, which she calls "the cold country." Inez is an extremely articulate person, deeply committed to working with grass-roots women—the classification she ascribes to herself. Most of her involvement is related to Puerto Rican women's participation in the Roman Catholic church. Inez likes herself and has a very healthy self-understanding. She has a college degree, has started her Master's Degree, and is in a job that combines both advocacy and service. She lives with her father—her mother died several years ago—in an apartment in the South Bronx, an area of New York City heavily populated by Hispanics.

When the group was asked if it wanted to talk in English or Spanish, Inez chimed in, "Español, por favor." This preference, to which the others agreed, reflects not only the fact that her Spanish is very good, but also that she sees speaking Spanish as a means of preserving her Puerto Rican roots, a means of self-identification for Puerto Ricans. For her to speak Spanish is a political action. She rarely talks in English or Spanglish.

Here is Inez's input.

My grandmother taught me the Hail Mary and the prayer to the Guardian Angel. My grandfather had made a promise to the Virgin of Mt. Carmel. In order to keep that promise, and also because in Puerto Rico there are many storms—to ask for her protection—every night my grandfather would light five candles.

At the beginning I thought that God was a punisher. I used to see him as a tall man, white, with a long, white beard. That was because my grandfather used to tell me that once when he died—he had been very sick—he went up there and the one that interviewed him had white hair. I always saw God as a punisher; I never saw him any other way. There he was looking, with a big book, writing down everything I did. In catechism classes they had told us hell was a huge cauldron with a clock in the middle that, instead of ticking, said, "You will never get out of here."

My grandparents made me pray the Hail Mary. We participated in the "Visits of the Virgin" [a statue of the Virgin is brought to visit your home and is kept there for a couple of days before moving on to another home]. They also participated in "Sung Rosaries." If they did that here, they would call the police because they do not just sing, they shout it! Neither my grandfather nor grandmother used to go to mass, but they would somehow get palms on Palm Sunday. . . . And I remember that if it thundered, my grandfather would light up a palm and would throw it outside because he thought that would make the thundering stop. Another thing that was very rooted in them was baptism. They used to say, "You have to pour water over the baby, or the baby will stay a Moor." [Since the Moors occupied Spain for centuries, in folk language the antithesis of Christian is Moor.] One of the reasons they did not take me to Puerto Rico until I was two months old was because they believed that one could not cross the sea without being baptized. . . . If you did not baptize the children, they were Moors and would go to limbo.

God was not important for them. They talked more about the Virgin of Mt. Carmel; in Puerto Rico she is someone so very special. They were always praying to her. The rosaries for the dead were always addressed to her. I do not remember them talking so much about God, only the phrase "God is going to punish you." And you made your First Communion because everyone made it, but there was not such a need for it.

I have never thought of describing God because for me it is not a person, it is like a *sentimiento* [deep feeling], a force that makes me move, which pushes me in difficult moments. It is a force, something I cannot explain. But if they would ask me to draw God, I would draw my grandmother smiling. Because she is the only person that I believe has filled me or filled me so much that I can compare her to God. I would draw a picture of my grandmother with her hands open, smiling, as if to say, "Come with me because I am waiting for you." God is strength for the *lucha* [struggle], strength to keep going ahead, to encourage. . . . For me it is always a force that moves me. And even if everybody would say that I am bad, that I cannot do it, that force says that I can do it, that I am special, that I am capable of moving mountains. But it is something outside of me that comes to me in the darkest and most difficult moments.

Look, I see Jesus as a perfect example of *lucha*, as a perfect example who broke with all the institutions and with everything that people followed. I see him as a person who, in difficult moments, I can sit down, read about, reflect on, and it gives me *animo* [encouragement] to continue. He suffered; he is a person I admire and contemplate. . . . Every person has leaders, and I think that he is the principal leader for me because of the life he led, because of how daring he is many times. And sometimes when I am in difficult circumstances, I say, "In similar situations, how would Jesus have acted?" And I use him as an example. . . . And one of the reasons I could not become a Marxist is because I did not see in Marx the qualities of Jesus, I did not see how he was going to transform my life. In spite of everything that happened in the convent, in spite of all I went through because of the novice mistress whom I wanted to murder—I never saw Jesus in what she did to me—I never broke up with God; I would tell him to give me strength. In spite of everything, that strength from God was what gave me *animo* to continue going ahead. . . .

Question: *That strength, is it part of Jesus?*

I think that Jesus has part of that strength, but no, when I think of that strength, I am not thinking about Jesus. I think about Jesus when I need a model for my life, a model for going ahead. I think that if it were not for the examples I see in the Gospels and what I hear the folk saying about Jesus. . . .

Question: *Do you pray to Our Lady of Providence?* [*This is the title under which Mary has been proclaimed patroness of Puerto Rico by the hierarchy of the Catholic church.*]

I do not know anyone who is called Providencia in Puerto Rico. In Mexico they are called Lupe [after Our Lady of Guadalupe] and in Santo Domingo everyone is called Altagracia [after Our Lady of Altagracia]. . . . But that thing about Our Lady of Providencia, that is new. [That is why no one is named Providencia.] I think that they needed someone so they could say they [the hierarchy of the church] have a Patroness, and they invented the thing about Providencia. They brought her from outside, nobody knows her. You know that is something very painful. You hear the Mexicans talking so much about their Virgin; the same with the Dominicans;[1] but not us, we are a colony. The Virgin did not appear to us, she came from outside, from Italy. [That is where the statue of Our Lady of Providence, which is in the cathedral in San Juan, came from.] The whole thing is very painful.

In difficult moments I pray to Jesus because I have him as my guide. But many times I do not dare to say this: I pray a lot to my grandmother. I do not know, look: I had a very beautiful experience. When she was dying, I went to the house of an aunt of mine. We were making oatmeal, I remember, it was five minutes to ten in the evening; we had a blackout, but the only lights that went off were the ones where we were. And I saw her in the screen door, and she said to me, "Inecin," that was her nickname for me, "I am leaving. Behave yourself, I am remaining with you." I started to scream, "My grandmother died, my grandmother died." My aunt told me to calm down, that it was not going to happen. Twenty-five minutes later all the cars that were at the hospital arrived, everyone with their heads down. . . . She never went away from me, she always stayed, and in the difficult moments I pray to her. . . . Sometimes I feel that her strength is so big, that I can get anything. . . . I never say it in public, but she is my favorite saint. The other ones, I respect them, but I never pray to them, only to her and to Jesus.

In my room I have a little statue of Our Lady of the Milk, but in his room my father has a big statue of the Virgin, and he has St. Jude, and no one can touch them, and he brings them flowers every Saturday.

Question: Regarding religion, are you the same or different from your parents and grandparents?

I resemble my grandparents a little because they had a lot of faith. It was not a faith based on the church, it came from within them; it was part of their culture, part of their life. My faith and my involvement with the church is because I *siento* [feel deeply] that it is part of my life, not because I follow many of the church's rules, because in reality I do not care. My grandparents did not go to mass, and I go when I have to go, but if I am very tired or I have something else to do, I do not go. The rules of the church did not matter much to them, and neither do they to me. I took in a lot of what today they call popular religiosity. The sense of God is a little bit different because I have never, never, never said that God punishes. I believe in a living God who, on the contrary, is there to help you, to *animarte* [encourage you], so you can keep going ahead; and all that he gives us are good things. I think that we punish ourselves by our own actions, and my grandparents thought, and so did my mother, that it is God who punishes. Many times I think that my mother did things for fear of God, not for love. And my experience is different. . . . But I think that if they lived now and would have had the opportunities that I had to learn certain things, they would follow my same line of vision and action.

My grandfather and my mother were strong. . . . My grandfather was like an Indian chief. . . . He was very polite with the people, but when he did not like someone, he would tell them. . . . What was for us pride in Puerto Rico has been a way of surviving here. . . .

Adela

Adela is a single mother of two and has a third child, not a blood relative, living with her. She was married in Mexico when she was very young, but that did not work out. The father of her two children is a man for whom she worked here in the United States. Adela has no legal American documents but seems to have first crossed into the United States about seven or eight years ago. At present, and for the last few years, she has been the cook in a parish rectory. Adela did not feel well during part of the meeting but remained with the group for the most part. She was rather quiet during the weekend; however, once she felt better, she engaged the other women when she did not agree with their opinions. She was also very capable of holding to her own opinions, even when several of the other women disagreed with her. Having been born and raised in Mexico, Adela speaks Spanish fluently and did not use English during the whole weekend.

What follows is her response to the questions about the women's understanding and sense of God.

My parents, both of them, were the ones who inculcated in me religion, and it goes on. Now I do it to my children. The first thing they taught me was to make the sign of the cross, the Our Father. For my mother the Our Father meant a lot because it was a prayer that asked for everything, "Give us this daily bread."

When I was small, my mother used to tell me: "Do not fight with your little brothers because, look, there is a God and there is a devil. When you hit your brother, God suffers and the devil gets very happy." And that is the same thing I tell my children now. . . . "Look, if you hit your sister it is as if you hit God." Because of this I became fearful—not afraid but a sense of respect, and I stopped fighting. If I was fighting with my brothers, God was crying and the devil was bursting out with laughter. Then I would tell myself, "No, you should not do it," because I knew that this God whom they had inculcated in me, I knew he was a good person, and I could not make that person who was good cry, while the other one, the devil, laughed. When my children fight, I tell them, "Look, you hit your sister, and God right now is crying, and the devil is laughing at you and is saying, 'Aha! I am winning you over.'" And they get scared just as I used to get scared. [She laughed after this last remark.]

I have one grandmother, but I think she does not even know that God exists. We have talked to her about that since she has been sick, because during her life she has been bad. She is Indian, *taraumara* Indian. And she is bad, she has black livers [an expression used to indicate how bad she is], because she has done many mean things to my mother, and my mother is very good—a person with a very big heart. We have tried to teach my grandmother to repent and to ask pardon of my mother for all the times she has offended her. And she says, "No, I cannot ask pardon of your mother because I am her mother." . . . My mother, she is the one who has taught us everything about religion. . . . They say that since I was born—I am the oldest—they went to mass, Sunday after Sunday. They used to take me to mass, and I grew up that way, every Sunday to mass. When my brothers were born, they also went, the whole family together. Now I am tired of being in church, and I do not go to mass. For me they were very good parents, and they inculcated in me many good things. My father does not live anymore, but I have my mother. My mother says that she started going to church on her own; in the ranch where she lived, they had catechists who came to teach them catechism once in a while. But my mother was a very bright person, and afterwards the catechist did not go to the ranch, and my mother was the one who started teaching catechism to the children in the ranch. And that is when she began to teach us. . . .

That first time I married, I was married by the church and by the civil authorities. No, my mother and my father were not opposed to the wedding. Well, I was not in love with my husband, but I was at the age that, like they say, "The bus is going to pass me by; I better get on it." Then my parents, they did not agree with my marriage, but more because of pride, they made me get married. Then my mother said, "Get married in the church." Well, I went to the church. I was in love at the moment but not enough to get married. Now I cannot get married in the church again.

I feel maybe less than my parents when it comes to religion, to what they taught me, because I do practice my religion but not like they taught me. I am less religious than what they taught me. First of all, I do not go to mass. I practice my religion in my house, but going to mass, no. Nor do I send my children. I send them to learn catechism, but not to mass. It is because the priests have hurt me so much that I do not believe them when they speak from the pulpit. They have hurt me so much, so much, that I do not accept them as teachers; they are lying, they are being hypocrites; no I don't believe them. And I can say it anywhere, that no, I do not go with those people. I prefer to practice my religion in my house. I do it many ways. I teach my children the Bible. I have started with my children from the first page. . . . I feel less religious than my parents because they did go to mass on Sundays, would go to communion and to confession. That is one thing; me, go to confession? No. Alone in my house I sit down and ask forgiveness of God; but I will not go to confession to a priest. There are many reasons for not going to a priest. Every day I sit down to eat with my children, and we thank God and we pray for all the people who have problems. My children now can sit at table, say a prayer without my saying anything, and ask God to help people who are having problems, the prisoners, those who have no food, those in war.

I have with me a girl who is now fifteen; she is with me since she was six or seven. My mother picked her up from a woman who did not care about her children. My mother said to me, "Look, if you want to do something, take that girl, because that girl is going to end up doing something that is not good." And I brought her, and she is with me; but I never have said that she is not related to me because many people could take advantage of her . . . so she is my niece, she is my same blood, and I protect her. But she is a very good girl, she is already fifteen; now this year we want to send her to school—see if we can. . . . She was also very, well, she did not know anything about God, she knew nothing about anything, she only lived, ate, and slept. The first time I sat her at table and started to talk with her, she was blank, because when I talk to my children, I talk to them the naked truth; I always have accustomed them to this—the good and the bad, they already know about it, even if they are small. But I *siento* [feel] good, I am well; who knows?

Question: How would you describe God to someone who has never heard about God?

I would look for a garden of only red roses and I would show it to him, and I would tell him that for me red roses mean very much, the most beautiful thing; with them I can show my love. I would paint for him a garden of red roses because I could not show him an image, or a cross with someone crucified because I do not know about what my ancestors have told me, the history of God dying on a cross. . . . [Adela did not finish this sentence. It is not clear what she was trying to say.] But I do know that God is love, and I can show how he has proved to me his love in so many ways. So I can show the stranger something that means love: a rose; a rose that signifies love. God takes care of me in all different ways, he has given me everything, everything, absolutely everything.

Jesus was a man who gave everything for us and came to give us life. I cannot say if he is God. I do not pray to Jesus.

Just now I had a very strong, very strong headache, and I said to Olga [one of the other participants], "Olga, I am going to ask the saint of your devotion that you have told us about, to see if he cures me." And the headache went away. I think this is good, is good, I do not know. Maybe he will be my new saint. . . .[2]

When I have a problem, I talk first to God. I do not ask any saint or anyone. And at times I find relief and at times no, but I resign myself.

I tell him, "Well, if this is the way you want it, let it be. But help me with this problem." And I have been able to go ahead, my problem has been solved. I have never doubted.

Question: When you asked that lady you were working for to return you to the Mexican side of the border and she did, but instead of $36 she gave you $5 for a week's work, did you pray? What did you do?

Well, I could not do anything, what could I do? But I learned; I did not feel anger, I did not feel anything because I could not do anything. With that $5 I went to a friend's house where I had left my clothes, but they had disappeared. According to her they had been taken. I decided I would return here, to the United States, and I said, "My God, help me." That same day I crossed the river back. I did not know anyone. I got together with some girls who worked in a saloon, and they started to teach me a little bit. Yes, I was a bit scared, but I had to work. But I only would ask God, "My God, help me, do not leave me, do not let me go, do not abandon me." And I made him thousands of promises. . . . Promises are promises, and I kept them. I have never doubted, and he is the only one I have asked, and I get ahead. It is what gives me strength, something happens, and I ask, and I get ahead . . . with God's help. They pay me $87 weekly, and they take away $7 and leave me with $80. With that I feed my children, I clothe them, entertain them; my only "vice" is going out to eat . . . going to eat at restaurants. . . . I do not know how, but I have enough for everything, many times even to lend money; and then, I even have money left in my purse, $30 or $40. If a problem arises, I am ready. I only ask God, and what I have lasts. I have never doubted God, that I remember. Any moment, wherever I am, I *siento* his presence. If I see a person in need, my heart aches, it hurts inside me. "If I have enough for my needs, why doesn't he?" . . . When bad things happen, instead of doubting God, I say, "Thank you, Lord, you know what you are doing." It means that he remembers you. One also needs once in a while to be reminded. . . .

When one asks God, I think that it is faith, faith in God, to ask him from inside, from the heart. Well, God hears us and gives us the means to be able to solve problems. But I ask him with all the faith I have; I do not ask him in a superficial way. I do not say, "My God, help me." No; I talk to him seriously: "Look, I know that I have gone as far as offending you, and I ask your pardon; I need you to help me. Forgive me for what has happened." But I ask him from inside; I do not ask him, "Come on, help me because I need you to help me." First, I analyze the time I have spent without talking to him. I say, "Ah, I know I have offended you, forgive me; and I need this." I think he helps us to solve things, he gives us the light we need.

I do not know if this is a foolish experience, but I think it was a crisis. My son Michael had encephalitis. When he was nine, for fourteen days he was between life and death, and the doctor told me that if he survived, his mind or some part of his body would be affected. But I asked God so very much, I asked him night and day, I did not eat, did not sleep, because I was suffering. I thought of throwing myself from the window of the hospital. My *patrona* [boss] said to me, "My child, give up [to God] Michael; why are you holding on to him?" Christmas was very close, and one night in the hospital, at two or three in the morning a man arrived, I do not remember his face. He arrived and knocked at the door of the room, and I thought it was a nurse. He asked me the name of my child, and I told him. He said to me, "Do you believe in God?" I said yes, and he said, "Don't worry, the 24th or 25th your son will be in your house with you." . . . Since then my faith has been reaffirmed more and more. I never saw the man again, and December 25th we were in the house of the *patrona* [where she was living]. . . . The doctor did find a bit of problem with my son's mind, but he has never been sick again. I find no way of explaining what happened. Many people might say, "Adela is crazy." But no, it is true. I never again saw that man; I do not understand who he was since at that hour the only ones around are nurses.

Marta

Marta was born and raised in Cuba. She was married in Cuba and has a son who married recently and a daughter who is finishing high school. In the early '60s she came to the United States as part of the large exodus of Cubans who left the island because of the Castro regime. She has been a single woman for the last six years. Marta pursues the managerial profession; she is a hardworking woman, highly motivated. She belongs to the so-called upper middle class: she lives with her family in a comfortable home, owns a boat, and often vacations away from the city where she lives.

Marta speaks a mixture of English and Spanish—a sentence might begin in English and finish in Spanish or vice-versa. Marta is extremely articulate and likes to express what she thinks, to grapple with it, and to be sure that she is communicating adequately what she believes. She went to an American high school in Cuba and has not pursued further studies.

Following is Marta's input.

In difficult moments I pray to God. I cannot tell you very precisely what he looks like. For me he is more a spirit, completely so. I do not dare to give him shape; he is prettier and more supreme the less shape I give him. I always refer to him in the masculine, he is father-looking—I mean he feels like a father more than looking like one. He is my father, my ultimate father. He is my protector who will do what is best for me.

I believe that God sent Jesus Christ and, because of what I was taught, which was deeply inculcated in me, I believe that God and Jesus are one and the same. Because of what I was taught, not because of what I feel, but because of what I was taught, for me they are linked, the two of them. Many times when I pray to Jesus Christ, he is the same as God, and in a way my mind links them together: God and Jesus Christ are one and the same. OK? He just took a form to come to earth.

More than in Jesus Christ as divine, I believe in Christianity as divine. I am at a point in my life where I doubt everything, and especially what I know. So I don't know and I don't believe in anything I thought I believed in. I cannot trust my beliefs, and I cannot any longer know what I know, and this is a conflict. But, what I do feel, not know, feel . . . I do believe in Christianity because it

makes sense to me. In this time of doubting everything, . . . I have
reverted back to my common sense and to what I feel. And Christianity does make sense to me, most of Christianity, and so, I believe in
Christianity. Not all of it perhaps, because I do not know all of it. But
what I know of it makes sense, is comforting, and I see it as a good
guideline for the human spirit. But I never pray to Jesus Christ. The
only time I do is perhaps in church, like during Holy Week or
something like that when you go through the suffering of Jesus
Christ. It is the same, you are praying to God. . . . But in moments of
danger, when you have to be able to count on someone, I pray to *Cheo*
[a nickname given to God, something like "Joe"]. And though I call
him *Cheo*, I always feel a little guilty, as if I were being disrespectful.

I used to pray to some saints, to St. Jude Thaddeus. When I was a
girl I had thousands of saints, I do not remember who they were. I
was very devout. I used to believe so much in promises that the time
came when I owed thousands of ejaculations;[3] a priest absolved me
from the obligation of saying them. If not, I would have had to spend
the whole day saying, "Jesus, Mary, and Joseph; Jesus, Mary, and
Joseph."

My favorite prayer was the Girl Scouts' prayer we said in Cuba. It
was so hard to live by it that I quit saying it. It says, "My God, teach
me to be generous, to serve you as you deserve, to give without
counting, fight without thinking of the wounds, and to give without
expecting any other recompense than to know that I am doing your
holy will." . . . For years I was able to say it that way; I then toned it
down. I cannot say it any longer; it is too high, too unattainable.

My mother has become more religious in the later years of her life.
I was the religious pillar of my house. My mother went to church so I
would not stop going . . . as a mother's duty . . . and the great fights in
my house were with my father, trying to convince him that he had to
believe. Mother would stay on the sidelines during the fights. She
never sided with me, and that is why I always say that she was not
that religious at that time, or maybe she did not want to tangle with
my father at that time and I did. . . . Daddy never, no, maybe once a
year, went to church. . . . Mom would take me to mass on Sundays,

Holy Week. I do not remember about when I was very small, but I do not recall going to mass with Mom until I started to go to Catholic school. . . . I would imagine that she did go to church, but, knowing my aunt and the family, they were not extremely religious. As I say, I believe that my mother has become religious; she got hooked on religion, and then she passed me and went ahead of me. I have stayed quite behind her.

I live my religion by being the most Christian I can be, starting with how I am at home and my behavior towards others, and with my children. I order my priorities so as to be a little bit like Jesus Christ rather than following church rules. In other words, I guide myself by the teachings regarding law and order, concern for others, justice and fairness—all of these things are Christianity, and if I do them unto those that I love, and even unto those that I don't love but that I think need my Christianity—to me that is my religion, more, much more, than going to church. I don't think that it is bad to go to church. And I feel guilty to a certain extent for not going to church because I think it is good to go to church to get those spiritual uplifts. It is just that I only have so much time, and since I don't believe I have that strong a need or need it anymore [to go to church]—I am religious in other ways: I need the time to see somebody, or I have to take care of my house, or go out in the boat on a family outing. The time I use that way is more important to me as an individual, as a spiritual person, and to me as a member of my family and for the rest of my family, than if I went to church. I do what I do, not to be a good Christian or because it is good for me, but because it is the expected behavior in order to emulate God and Christ and to be the way I feel religion calls me to be. I do it, not to please myself, but to be the best me I can possibly be. That is my religion to a certain extent.

I never read the Bible. Once in school I had a Bible class, and it was just like any other subject, like you read a history book. I only know the passages that are read at mass on Sundays. And I do not have the least idea of what is the Old Testament. Bible to me is an unknown subject. I was taught religion more through feeling and example. I remember my Bible, they made us buy it one year, and we read it a couple of times. We took a history of the Bible course, things related to God. My nuns taught me religion through their own stories. They reminded me very much of what Christ did with the apostles, that he sat with them and told them stories; that is how I was taught religion; they lived it; they ingrained it in me. All that about reading the Bible is very American. In Cuba the Bible was not important.

Lupe

Lupe is a Mexican American who has lived all her life in the Southwest. She is the oldest of a large family, and she helped her parents raise her younger brothers and sisters in many different ways, including financially. She finished her college education when she was older, is now married, and has no children. Lupe is a business-woman in an important corporation that directly relates to grassroots people. Her job has brought her much visibility, and, being very civic-minded, she has become involved in many community activities. This is also because she has always been very active in the church, about which she is very knowledgeable. Lupe is articulate and has grappled repeatedly with the issues she talks about here. Several times she indicated that her understandings about a certain issue are only in process—that what she was sharing was only the beginning of an answer. Lupe spoke mostly in English, using Spanish only for emphasis or to quote others, especially her parents.

Here is Lupe's input.

My grandmother was a very religious woman. In the family she was the epitome of faith, the epitome of religion. And that was so not only in my family but in the community—that is still true. My first memory of praying is of going with my grandmother to visit people in the community. She helped others, went to be with others. I also used to fall asleep listening to my mother praying the rosary and unending litanies. Her praying was like a lullaby. The prayers came from my mother, and also she taught me the importance of patience. Her sense was that if you prayed for something, that was something important, or you would not be praying for it.

The first prayer I learned was to make the sign of the cross and to ask for bread. They would simply tell us to ask for bread and we would. I do not remember my father praying like my mother did, but he is a very nonverbal person, and his faith is very much linked to who he is and the work he does. My father was a laborer and was very proud of that. He always told us, "When you fill out the applications, be sure that you write that I am an unskilled laborer." He felt honored by what he did. He would borrow a car—we did not have one—and he would tell us, "Look, I am going to take you to see all the buildings your father has made." Now, as an adult, I have learned that the virtue that best describes my father is meekness.

Very early on I separated the religion of my home from what the church taught me. The priests in my church were Spaniards, but what they said was not the real thing for me. The world of prayer at the house was separated from the church. It was very frustrating for me as a little girl because I went to church and heard what they said, and then I had inside the other me. My grandmother was also very involved with the church. She organized singlehandedly the *viejitas* [an endearing term for "old women"], and they all made and sold enough *tamales* to build two different churches. Even to today the *viejitas* are doing the same sort of thing.

Question: What image of God do you have?

I am so sure that there is a God! God for me is like a composite of the qualities I admire in other people and which I myself want to have. I talk to him, and he talks back to me in things that happen to me. I call them "miracles." Let me give you an example of what I mean.

The company I work for had a very important business matter to transact in Wall Street. So I went with a group of my peers, and, on the way there, they pointed out to me that I was the senior partner of the group and that, therefore, I had to head this delegation. I said, "Oh, sure." But to myself I said, "Oh, my God, what am I going to do?" In New York we were staying in a plush hotel, and I was a nervous wreck because in the company I deal more with services than with the financial aspect of the business. Anyway, the night before the meeting, I read everything in the packet that the company had put together, and, though I was very nervous, I knew I could not ask any one of my peers. I did not want to lose face with them as a woman and a Mexican American—so if I was in charge of the group, I was supposed to know!

We were to be in Wall Street on Wednesday at 10 A.M., and I did not remember what Wednesday it was or anything. St. Patrick's Cathedral is next to the hotel, so I said to myself, "I am going to get up early, get all dressed up, put on my make-up and go to St. Patrick's." So I went, and it was Ash Wednesday.[4] Many times I do not take the ashes because I get disgusted at the lines in the churches, all the people who never go to church, men who beat up their wives—and they go to get ashes. So I go to St. Patrick's, and I was not going to get *cenizas* [ashes]. But then I felt I had to go. Then I asked myself if I was going to go to Wall Street with *cenizas*. I said to myself, "Lupe, are you ashamed of *cenizas*?" Somehow getting *cenizas* became such an important thing to me that I had to get them. I had gotten up early in the morning so I had time to stand in line, and I got *cenizas*.

I then went back to the hotel and ate the $24 breakfast—quite a price, no?! And then I felt really good. I said to myself, "These people cannot possibly expect me to be an expert on the technicalities; I think all I need to do is talk about our company and the need for cooperation." So I had in mind what I was going to say at this meeting. And we got there and sat in this room with this huge table and waited because the main person to whom we were supposed to talk was not there. Then he walked in, and in the middle of his forehead were *cenizas*! We looked at each other and smiled and sat down. He and I connected immediately; nobody else but the two of us had *cenizas*. And everything in the meeting went on fine, and we got good results. This is the kind of happening that I call "my miracle"—God talking to me, being with me.

So many times it is like that. I have no idea of what to do or what to say, and somehow I still do it or say the right thing—it is wonderful. I sit with the people, with the *viejitos*, with a woman who has been beaten by her husband—there is a lot of pain, and it seems to me that God is more where there is pain. God is there. I am not the one who is doing things for the people; it is God doing for the people. I find appropriate words to say—but they are not my own words; many times they are beautiful words from church songs, like "Be Not Afraid."[5] But God is there; I have no idea what he looks like. He is there, all over. Those happenings that I know are a result of God being there—that's faith, and that's God. That makes up for all the *apachurrones* [being stepped on] and all the confusions and all the hurts and all the unanswerable questions. Those kinds of moments, the "miracle moments," are many—though not always frequent.

Jesus, I don't know; it's like this, Jesus is in the Bible, and he is God's pilot project, you know? God does not have an image or anything; so if I need to imagine God, well I can think of Jesus. Jesus is a pilot project because he had to do something and he did it; but look what happened to him! I don't pray to Jesus, but he is with me—we are getting *cachetadas* [slaps in the face] together and *aplastones* [crushings] together. He is like a partner or a brother, someone who is with me. He has qualities that I admire, like if you do something good, you do not talk about it, you do not brag about it; if someone does something bad to you, well, you turn the other cheek; you do not push yourself on people; you are humble. God is something else; God is the one that is making everything happen; he is bigger, and that is why I ask him to take away my being afraid in certain circumstances or give me more courage. Jesus hurt, but God is almighty, is everywhere, can do everything. In time of real need my prayer starts always, "Oh my God." I am calling on the big one, the Almighty One.

Question: What about Mary?

In school everything was Mary, Mary! She has changed complexion as I have gotten older. I could identify with her because of her faithfulness. Now, since I started working with the community, the Virgin of Guadalupe has gotten more important. When I was little, I heard all the time in my family the invocation, "Holy Virgin of Guadalupe." They said it for everything. The Virgin of Guadalupe, I think, comes the closest to giving my Christian womanhood the dignity that it needs. I pray to her because the Virgin of Guadalupe is *morena* [brown-skinned], the Virgin of Guadalupe is a mother, she is a pregnant woman, she is an Indian woman, and she spoke to Juan Diego—she understood the Indians and their needs; that the miracle of her apparition took place, well, that historically changed a nation!

Question: Do you read the Bible; is it important to you?

I do not read the Bible that much. But I absolutely hate the readings that are used for the wedding ceremony—I think it comes from Paul—that the wife should be submissive to the husband. It is chauvinistic; it is terrible! Also, I as a woman who does not have any children, I feel real bad about the reading that talks about the wife having all those children who will sit around the table. It's like telling me that I am not holy; I don't like it. Those readings demean women. I like some Old Testament stories. I like the Book of Job a lot. And who was the one who was swallowed by the whale? Jonah? I like that story a lot also. I also like Ruth.

María

María was born in Puerto Rico but was brought to the United States when she was very small. She was the youngest of eleven children, and her mother gave her to an aunt to bring up. María married and had twelve children; three died when they were young. She is involved in church affairs in her area and also in politics. She has been district leader and also has been elected to the school board. Though she now lives by herself—her husband died of cancer—she is very close to her children and travels to different cities in the United States where they now live. María speaks both English and Spanish; during the meeting she spoke Spanish. She is very articulate, and she speaks calmly but is certain of what she says. She is in her early 60s and sees herself continuing to be involved in community affairs for some more years.

Here is what she said regarding her understanding of and relationship with God.

The aunt who brought me up was the one who first spoke to me about God, but I do not remember it as being at a very early age. I was already older. In reality, I always suffered very much because my mother did not raise me; and I never was able to understand that. When I learned that there is a God and could see pictures of this being—the pictures of God they show the children—this image became my refuge in my moments of sadness. I really do not remember who taught me to pray, but the first prayer I learned was the Hail Mary.

I saw God as a compassionate being because in my childhood I suffered so much, I suffered so much. My aunt had been married for ten years, and she had no children so she took me and brought me up. After she took me, then she got pregnant and had a daughter. And, naturally, the world just flowered for her, and she gave all her love to her daughter. She gave me all I needed materially, but that motherly love—no, I never knew it. God became that love of a mother and a father that I never had. I cannot say anymore, or I will start crying.

My aunt was a good woman, but she was obsessed with spiritism.[6] She would take me to spiritist centers, and in the house she would spend her time reading the cards; this was even a source of income for her, I think. I know that people used to come to the house to consult with her. So my early youth was full of spiritism. My aunt was good; she always said, "Do good regardless of who benefits from it."

I did not get any of the ideas I now have about religion at my home. You know, after all that I saw there, I have never believed in any of the things that spiritism taught. I used to see the women that would come there to consult my aunt—such idiots. They believed all the foolishness my aunt would tell them—what she would read in the cards. And I saw the absurdity of it all. I never was able to accept that sort of thing and believe in it. I remember years later when my husband was dying of cancer, a woman told me to take him to a spiritist. I just could not do it. A relative of mine took him and gave him the baths that the spiritist recommended. Not me!

It was a neighbor who gave me my first sense of the church. It seems she would ask my aunt permission to take me to catechism lessons and to mass. And I liked it. I liked it so much that when I was a little bit older, I would go to mass alone. And they would say, "She's like her grandfather," because he used to go to mass every day. But I never met him. Like always, in church I was searching for a maternal or paternal image. And in God I found that image, that love that I felt I did not have in my home. I found it in the picture of Christ with the beard and the beautiful face. And I remember that I used to cry when I was small . . . and I still cry. Maybe that is why I had so many children, and I wanted to give them all that love that I did not have when I was a child.

I am totally different from my aunt, whom I called Mom. I did not have those beautiful religious teachings that I hear other women talk about. I was searching for a crutch—something that would help me because as a child I knew that I was missing something. I dove into the church searching there for what I was missing. My religious formation was something I provided for myself; they did not give it to me; I went after it as a lifesaver.

. . . In 1954 my first son died. . . . Once life started banging me up with his death, then I had to look for something that would alleviate my pain. And there is where I really started my involvement. I always went to church, I was Catholic by birth,[7] went to church on Sundays, and that was the end of that. But after I had this suffering so big, I realized that I had to hold on to something because, if not, I was going to go crazy; and that is when I started getting involved and belonging to some church-affiliated organizations. . . . In 1967 and 1968 I lost two other sons. . . . That is when I got totally involved in the church; all the paths that opened up—there I was. I used to tell myself, "The people must say that I am like white rice, mixed in with everything." I was looking for something. My children were already grown; some of them were married. They were going on with their lives, and I had to go on with mine. In spite of having such a big family, I knew that I was missing something. My husband was a typical Puerto Rican: very quiet, very reserved, very, very much of a man, a bit domineering. But he always was a bit understanding, and he did not oppose a lot my getting involved in politics. . . . After I finished my two terms in office, I left politics and got involved in other things as leader. . . . In 1980 I lost my husband, and I then said to the Lord, "Well, now I am totally yours, and you can use me as you please." As soon as I said this to the Lord, I started receiving so many invitations to participate—of course, in church-related events and groups. At times I have gone to eighteen meetings in a week! I work in a school where I have the opportunity to help with the needs of our community . . . and I always imagine that God is using me because I always find an opportunity to help, to do good. I feel now that the tragedies in my life prepared me for this—to be alone, to do so much outside my home; my life is so full, I do so very much.

I see God as a brother, as a friend, as a father, as a mother, as a supernatural force. I am confident that God[8] is with me always; the more down I feel, it is as if a supernatural force would lift me up; it gives me positive ideas on how to keep going; this force helps me to realize that I am not alone. No matter how alone I am, no matter how much it seems to me that the whole world is falling on me, and that maybe I have no other means, no doors to open, that all the doors are closed, I feel something that, at times I say, speaks to me. Especially when I am lonely, which is when one thinks about one's sufferings and problems the most, something places the thought in my mind that I can do it, that this is the road that I have to follow, or this is what you have to do in order to struggle with what is happening to you. There is a very beautiful picture, like this, with lowered head. There are also some words on the picture, but I do not remember the words right now. The attitude is one of thinking and suffering, and I see him as if thinking about so many problems which all of us throw on top of him . . . trying to find a solution to these problems.

Question: If you were a painter, how would you paint God?
I would definitely paint him as an extended hand, ready to lift up,

to lift up whoever goes his way. We fall physically and spiritually; that hand resembles what happens when you fall in the street, and someone comes to help you get up. I see it as the hand that gets you up, and it gives you the strength to keep going ahead. I see him as a tremendous inspiration in my life; I see him as a son. I love the beautiful relationship he had with his mother—like the one I had with my children. Especially in the first miracle which he made because his mother asked him.

Question: That hand then is the hand of Jesus?

Yes. That relationship that he had with his mother when she asked him at the wedding at Cana to do something because there was no more wine. And he says to her, "What do you want me to do?" He listened to his mother. His mother asked him something, and he could not deny her petition, he could not turn his back—and he did his first miracle. I love that relationship between him and his mother because I see him being so human, and she is also so human as a mother. . . . I see him as very real, as a figure to which I can relate.

I see him as my equal because he came here and was among us. He created us in his image and came here and went through all the sorrows we go through. That is why I like the picture of him being so pensive; because we know, we have read, that he suffered just as we do. That makes me be on very familiar grounds with him. When I suffer much, I think, "But he suffered so much and through no fault of his own." At times I say, "My God, why do I have to suffer so much? Do I merit such suffering? I am not that bad of a person." But I will never be as perfect as he was. Yet, he suffered and suffered, and he was able to stand the suffering—just like me. And I identify myself with the Virgin; she suffered so much for him. And, as a mother, the largest portion of my suffering is because of my children.

In difficult moments I pray a lot to God. My problem in life is my children. Now I have a son who is in prison—buried alive. There is nothing worse for a mother than to see a son suffering. . . . I do not know from where I have drawn strength. My prayers are not prayers anymore, but I shout and I beg and I supplicate and I anguish. The last thing I do before going to bed is to pray for my children and my grandchildren, and especially for him who needs it the most. I pray to God, but my need, because of this son of mine, is so big that I send every single saint I find to intercede with God in favor of my son. I have special devotion to St. Martin de Porres—I am madly in love with that lovely black man because of a special favor I asked him once, and he answered me right away. Also the Virgin Mary; I think that the relationship between Mary and her son is so intimate that anything we ask her, she is going to talk to Jesus about it, and he is going to listen to his mother, and we are going to get it.

In my daily journeying I pick up all the saints that people recommend to me. For example, I worked in the centennial celebration of the Church of Our Lady of Mt. Carmel. . . . Now I take her by the hand, and I send her to Jesus with my message. St. Lawrence —whom the Mexicans say is the saint of miracles—I also picked him up.

I see God helping me, helping me in the strength that he gives me. The second time my son was put in prison, I wanted to get out of everything I was involved in; my pain was so great . . . I just wanted to give up. . . . But he needs me more than anyone else. So I know that God has given me the strength. And there are people in the church who have known me for many years, and they have seen all that I have had to go through, and they say to me, "You have your place in heaven secured because you have gone through all the bad things here in this earth, and God sends you all these things because he loves you." And I at times think, "My God, if you please would not love me so much." Other people tried to get me away from the church. They said to me, "You should get out of all the church affairs in which you are involved. How is it possible that so many difficult things come your way when you are so dedicated to church work? Maybe all this involvement is not what God wants from you." But I said to them, "If God did not want me doing all that I do, he would not give me all the opportunities to get involved. The Lord has me where he wants me."

I have not doubted my faith, but I have questioned it. When my son went to prison . . . I said to God, "I have served you, Lord, and not because I wanted you to reward me." Because I feel I already have received so much in my life. My children are so good. . . . And there are many people who love me. Each day I find out that I have more. But I have questioned my faith. I do not think I am a saint, but I am a good person, human, who cannot see someone in need without trying to help that person. "Why can't I have peace?" I have asked myself time and again, because one cannot have a son who is suffering and be at peace. And I know that the questioning is wrong, but it is so human to do that.

God is so busy, and, of course, I would like him to take care of me first, I would like him to put the rest of the world "on hold" until he took care of me. I send the Virgin, all the saints I find along the way, to see if they can influence God. The same with Jesus; there are so many people asking him. But, as the saying goes, "God does not give us what we ask but what is good for us."

Yes, I have a crucifix in my house and statues of all the saints that I pray to. I also wear medals of Christ and of the Virgin.

I like very much the Scripture passage that says, "I was in prison and you visited me." And I like it not only because I have a son in prison but because I think that many of us Catholics spend our time beating our breasts, spending our time in church, claiming that we are this and we are that, that we belong to this group and this other organization. But next to us we find a person who seems to be dead, and we do not do anything. I think that one of the things that God asked us so many times was that we love our neighbor as ourselves.

Olivia

Olivia is a Texas-born Mexican American who moved to the Midwest twenty years ago. She has been married twenty-nine years and has two sons and a daughter. Only the youngest son, twenty years old, lives at home. The other two are married and have given her four grandchildren. Olivia has never worked outside the home since she got married.

At present Olivia volunteers to teach religion to children in her church. She also takes communion to shut-ins. She would like to be more involved in ministerial work but, up to now, has not found a way to do it. For a short time she was in a program that trains lay ministers, but that did not work out satisfactorily. But it is her sense of ministry that pushes her to be available to help her neighbors and friends.

Olivia is the quiet type but speaks with great conviction. Because her group was rather large, there was not as much time to go into all the different themes as there was with other groups. Some of the things Olivia said seemed incomplete when the proceedings of the gathering were transcribed. Olivia was contacted, and on the telephone she clarified and amplified some of her answers.

When Olivia was asked to share something about her life, she shared very little factual information. Instead she related how about six years ago she came to realize that she needed to do something for herself.

I felt empty. I knew that I had to bring up my family, and I have my husband who is a very good man. But I knew I was missing something. I would ask myself, "What is happening to me?" When I prayed, I knew something was happening to me; I felt empty, but I did not know what it was that I needed. I was living like the shut-ins because I was concentrating only on my family. So I asked myself, "What am I going to do? What does God want me to do when my children grow up and live apart from me? What is it that I have to do for myself, to help myself?" It was then that I started discussing things with my husband. . . . He did not understand, he did not want to hear. But, a step at a time, with a lot of prayers, I kept thinking about how could I share my faith with others, how I could help others and at the same time help myself. When I started visiting old folks, they were very happy to see me; but it is also true that I would come back home full of energy. . . . Little by little I worked on developing myself under God's guidance. Then I joined the Ministry Program. . . .

It was all a matter of asking myself, what was I going to do when the children were gone and I had more time? I was not going to stay home cleaning the same little bit of space all the time. I kept wondering how I could help myself. And when we went to class, my husband went with me; that helped us a lot. I would explain to him that God was calling me to help others, not so much for their sake, but for my own sake. In the Ministry Program I learned I by myself am a person, without needing to be attached to another one to be of worth; then I read in Scripture about the fact that when we face God, he is going to ask me about myself, and I will not be able to use my husband, my children, as an excuse for what I have done or have not done. I am going to have to be accountable for myself and what I have done. My participation in the Ministry Program was very important for my own development. It did not work, partly because the supervisor we had was not good, but I told him, "I have to drop out of this program, but I will never stop being involved in the ministry of God." . . .

My grandparents were the ones who set an example for me when I was young. In a very special way I have to mention an uncle of mine. He never married; he was blind in one eye and saw just a little out of the other. In the house my mother had an altar, my grandmother had an altar . . . and when this uncle would wake up, the first thing he would do was to pray. And I was very curious and was always asking questions, and I would ask him, "Uncle, what are you doing?" And he would explain to me how to start off his day, first of all he was talking to God. When it came time for breakfast, which was nothing elegant because we were very poor, I would notice that, even if all he had to eat was a tortilla or a piece of bread with his cup of coffee, he would not put anything in his mouth before asking for God's blessing. Even when it was only *frijoles*—that is what we ate every day, and I would get tired of eating *frijoles*, but he would say, "No, my child; we have to give thanks to God for whatever we have to eat. If it is just a little—then we thank God for that."

The example my grandmother, my mother, this uncle gave me was of having faith in God; they always hoped that one day it would be better for us. Maybe they would not see those better times, but the younger ones would. And that influenced me a lot. I used to think, "One day I will be able to eat a bologna sandwich," which was a

great thing for me when I was little. I always was thinking about food
. . . and I would follow my uncle around all the time. He would go
apart and meditate, and there I was asking him, "What are you
doing?" And he would tell me. He got sick one day and died that very
same day.

My sense of God when I was small was that God was always with
us—even if we could not see him—he was with us, taking care of us.
That gave us strength to go on, to believe that even if we only had
frijoles or potatoes, we would not starve to death.

My mother did not go to church on Sundays because she did not
have a good dress, and she said the people would criticize her and talk
about her. But she would send all of her children to the catechism
classes in church. When we would go to my grandmother's house, she
would sprinkle us with holy water, asking for God's blessing. My
uncle was the one who taught me the sign of the cross. That was when
I was very small. Then when I went to catechism classes—that was
very important. There I learned the Our Father and the Hail Mary.
And the nun was very strict. She taught me, and I am grateful for
that, that when I was in church, it was only a matter of myself and
God. And that has stayed with me even to today. When I made my
First Holy Communion, it was very important for me. God was now
in a very real sense with me.

I always think of God and Jesus together. I know that they are not
the same, but when I say God, I refer to both. I see God as a
man—because that is the way God is pictured. A very special man
who is a true friend. When at times we feel that he is not listening—it
is not like that. For me he is a person in whom one can trust, a person
to whom one can say what one would not share with anyone else. And
you can share like that because he already knows before you say it. In
my experience, I have noticed and learned that he likes for us to go to
him. He is there always, always. We might believe that at times he is
not there, but that is not so. I feel such peace, such happiness when I
feel his presence in me. To symbolize him I would draw a mother
with her child. You know how when a child hurts his hand and the
mother kisses the little hand, the child feels all better? That is the way

I feel when I talk with him; I feel like a child who goes to him, and by the time I finish talking to him, I know that things are already better. I also see God in others, in the sick people, in those who need help. If someone telephones me and says to me, "Listen, I did not have enough money to buy bread"; then you have to tell that person, "I have one—I'll bring over half for you." In that kind of situation it is God who is letting me know, seeing if I can share what God has given me. This happened to me a couple of weeks ago. A friend called me and said she had to go to the eye doctor and did not find out until that day that they were going to put some drops in her eyes and that she would not be able to drive herself back home. She needed someone to take her. I said to her, "Don't worry, I will take you." In small things like this is when I see God. That is how I would paint him.

Question: You say that the image you have of God is a male image, but the examples you give us are of females: a mother, you helping a woman friend. Can you talk about that?

Because the love of a mother is something very special. Scripture quotes God, "Even if your mother forgets you, I will not forget you." . . . We have to trust God the way a child does. . . .[9]

I have a lot of faith in the saints. I see them as persons who are very special in the eyes of God. I know who they are and who God is; I do not place them higher than God. They gave themselves totally to God; everything they did was for God. If only I could have a little of what they had, to tolerate frustrations and keep going ahead. They did so many good things for the people. I do not do it every day, but at times I start to pray, and I name all the saints, Saint Thérèse, Saint Anthony, Saint Martin de Porres, Saint Jude. Yes, I do have faith in them.

When something happens and I start to pray, the first thing I say is, "My God, give me strength." I ask for myself so that then I can help others.

When I realized I had to change my life and begin to take care of myself, I wanted to do things my way. It did not work. Then I began to listen more carefully to what God was saying, "You have to do it my way and not your way." From then on, every day I would say,

"Show me what I have to do today to help myself and help my family." And little by little my husband has changed. . . . God sends trials, but God knows what he is doing. No matter what happens, I say, "I have faith in you." I have faith, and God is going to win.

I am the same as my parents and grandparents in thinking that God is always with me, taking care of me. I always say that I am eighty percent old-fashioned and twenty percent modern. I am not closed to modern ideas. For example, my two married children got married in the Baptist church because they were afraid of the classes that the Catholic church makes them take as marriage preparation. They were afraid they would not pass those classes. Well, where they get married is their problem; my problem is accepting. I even cooked for the two hundred people that came to the wedding. If I were totally old-fashioned, I would have said to them, "Once you go outside my religion the doors are closed." But for me, faith, the way God helps me to understand what faith is, is to teach his love; so if I had not accepted their marriages, then I would not be teaching them the love of God, and if I do not teach my own children, how am I going to teach those outside my home? At first I would not accept it, but after asking God what he would do if he were in my situation, I accept it.

Before, I never read the Bible, but after I started to search how to become myself, I read the Bible every day. I am now trying to memorize some of the psalms. I like especially the Good Shepherd Psalm. I cannot think offhand of any text that I do not like or have difficulty with.

Margarita

Margarita is a Cuban who has lived in New York City for many years. She came here about forty years ago to "see if I could get ahead in life." She married a man born in the United States of Cuban parents and had twins, one now a grown-up father of six children, and the other a daughter who still lives with Margarita. Margarita is a licensed practical nurse at a hospital, a job she has had for many years. She is deeply religious and enjoys talking and sharing her experiences and points of view.

I come from a family of eight. I have a sister here, and the rest of the family is in Cuba. I had an aunt who lived here, and I decided to come to the States. I tried to go back when my mother was very sick, but I was not able to. I have never gone back to Cuba.

When I was young in Cuba, after grade school, I started to study typing, but what I really liked was to sew and to help the old folks. I just would help anyone I could in my neighborhood; I would help the sick; I would go to church to get the priest to bring communion and give the sacrament of Extreme Unction to the sick. I would also collect the names of people in the neighborhood who were not baptized and would take them to the priest. As you know, in Cuba the priest would come to the different neighborhoods to baptize those who had not received the sacrament. That is what I liked to do. I was a member of two associations, The Sacred Heart of Jesus and The Sacred Heart of Mary. The Association of the Sacred Heart of Mary would organize this huge procession of Our Lady of the Unprotected only every twenty-five years. They would organize the procession when there was great need in the country. I only saw the procession one time when I was small. It was such an enormous affair. I do not know if you remember, but shortly after the procession it started to rain; it rained very much. And then the United States government sent economic aid to Cuba. I was also there when they crowned Our Lady of Charity as Patroness of Cuba. I was part of a huge choir that sang in that occasion. We were given these beautiful white uniforms. It was the most beautiful thing in my life; it was so very emotional . . . when they brought from El Cobre [the town where the statue of Mary is kept] to Santiago Our Lady to have her crowned. Because they always say that the Virgin should never be taken out of El Cobre.

My mother taught me how to pray. The first prayer I learned was the sign of the cross. I went to a small private school because my father wanted us to learn English—he thought that was very important. At this small school every morning we said prayers—the Our Father and the Creed. Since the time I was very small, I liked the church very much. I would get up very early every morning, at five in the morning, and would go in the darkness of dawn to the church. I would go with a friend. My mother had to stay at home to take care of the younger ones. I would go one morning to one church, the next morning to another one. I learned this from my mother; she was very religious and also my father who obliged us to go to church on Sundays. We would go to catechism on Saturdays and then to the religion classes in another church on Sunday. I liked it so very much. I received my First Holy Communion in one church and was confirmed a couple of weeks later in the other one.

In my house we prayed every night. My mother would say every night, "We have to pray in this house, we cannot go to bed without praying because God is the only one who gives us life, who gives us everything. God is nature, and we have to respect him." My father obliged us to pray. In the house we would pray the Our Father, the Hail Mary, the Creed. The rosary—I used to go in the evening to a church to say the rosary. This was when I was very young, seven or eight years old. I was always in church when my friends would come looking for me at home. My friends would be sent to church to find me. The processions of Good Friday were magnificent. I would always participate. The statue of Mary, the Sorrowful Mother, would leave from one church, and the statue of Jesus in the Sepulcher would leave from another one. It was indescribable what I felt when the two processions would meet. Just talking about it gives goose bumps. Even today when Good Friday comes around, I wish I were in Santiago.

When I was small, I would ask my mother where God was. She would tell me, "God is here, is everywhere. You do not see him but you can feel him. When you go to church, you do not see God, but you receive the host, and God is in the host." I used to be worried about chewing the host because the nuns and the priests would tell us not to. And my mother agreed with them. "Do not chew the host because God is in it." I asked the nun about faith. I knew that, according to the definition in the catechism, faith is to believe what one does not see. She asked me if I believed in God, and when I said I did, she said, "Then you have faith because you believe but you do not see God. It is just as with the air. You do not see it, but you know that it is there. When you were born, you were just a physical body, but God breathed into you the spirit, and then you became a person."

I always wanted to be like Mary; but the nun told me never to say that because we were all sinners, and we could not be identical to Mary; we can follow in her footsteps but never be exactly like her. But my idea about God was that he is something much more powerful than we are; we see the trees growing, and we cannot make them grow. And that beautiful sky, we did not make it. And my mother would always say, "There is something much more powerful than us."

In reality, I wanted to be a nun, but you know how things were, it was not possible to be a nun if you were poor. I feel that the changes that have occurred in the lives of the nuns are not for the better. I think that once the nuns give their word to God, they should not leave the convent and get married. If she wants to get married, then she should not have given herself totally to God. I find it very hard when people from other religions talk bad about the Catholics because of what the nuns do. Yes, I have friends from other religions, I visit other churches, and when they invite me, I go with them. Last weekend I went to Washington with the Church of God. I go for the trip; I have a friend in that church that has come to the Catholic church, and she invites me.

I have no concrete visual picture of God. I would describe him to someone who does not know anything about him as the Supreme One, the only powerful one, the one who does everything, who can do everything, the one who gives us life, and the one who takes it away from us. He is the only one, he could do away with the sun if he wanted to. Christ is the Son of God, the one who came from the Father, who became man to live among us. Looking at the Son, Christ, we can describe the Father because God made man in his image . . . so God must be something like Christ but much more superior. The Son came to tell us, "I am the Son of God, through me you will be able to go to the Father." I see God spiritually, I do not imagine, I cannot describe him. I see God more abstractly, spiritually.

It is like space, like the air we breathe, which we cannot see but we know is among us. The same with God, he is among us, but we cannot see him because he is so supreme, so infinite, that we do not see him.

How God works is a secret, and, according to the book I am reading, we should not try to learn those secrets. We do not know how it is that he relates to us who as humans are limited. We should not try to delve into mysteries. The book is *The Imitation of Christ* by Kempis; and there it says that we should leave the mystery of God alone. My mother used to say to me, "The only one who knows the secrets of God is his son Christ; not even the Virgin Mary knew the secrets of the Celestial Father." Many times I wanted to ask questions, and my father would not let me.

Mary for me is just great. Many people say me, "You Catholics believe in so many Virgins!" I explain that it is one Virgin who appears in different parts, and then we call the one person by different names. We have but one Mary who is the Mother of God. She is the most delicate woman, the sweetest, the one who was born without sin. She was preserved to be the mother of God, she is the biggest thing in the world. She is a model for me; but who can be like Mary? It is not possible; we sin with our thoughts, with our words, with our looks—we sin every way in our lives. One time when I was in church, I decided to go around and pray in front of the different statues. This priest came by and said to me, "You are stupid, praying to these statues made of plaster. They do not answer you, right? They have lips but do not talk, hands but do not act, feet but do not walk. They cannot answer you. When you come to church, pray before the Blessed Sacrament; there is where God is; he is the only one who can answer you." I thought about it, and I think he was right; people go into church and pray in front of the statues of the saints and ignore the Blessed Sacrament. So when I pray in front of a statue of Mary, I always first ask pardon of God, and then I say, "Dear Virgin, I stand here, but I do not talk to this statue but talk to you who are spiritually among us." The statues are only a reminder. The people like statues because they can see them, and they cannot see God who is spiritually present among us.

For me, the only saint I pray to is Mary, under the invocation of Our Lady of Charity, the title given to Mary in Cuba. I pray to her and to the Son, Jesus Christ. Our Lady of Charity takes care of me and of Cuba. If she was able to save the three men she appeared to who were about to perish in that little boat, she can save me and can save Cuba. The thing is that we have to be punished for all the innocent blood that has been shed since the time of our war of independence. And until those sins are paid for—it might well take several generations—the promise Mary made about Cuba will not become a reality. That promise is that Cuba will be cleaned of all sins, to set it free as before; she is our banner.

In difficult times I pray to God first of all; then I pray to the Sacred Heart of Jesus and to the Blessed Virgin Mary. I always invoke the Sacred Heart, ask him to help me and my family. In those difficult moments I always say, "My God, let it be done according to your will." But the truth is that when my mother was sick, I did rebel against God. I had the picture of my mother in my Bible, and I took it out. Then I was sorry and put it back in, and I asked pardon of God for that every day. It really hurt me that she died, and I was not able to see her.

The Bible, the truth is that I do not always read it. Sometimes I read the Bible, and then I go for two or three weeks without reading it. But I do read books like *The Imitation of Christ* and also this big book of meditations on Mary—it is like her biography.

Recurring Themes

In trying to bring together the understandings of these women, certain key words are used repeatedly and/or given great emotional emphasis.

Promesas (promises)

Inez speaks of how influenced she was by the promises made by her grandfather to the Virgin of Mt. Carmel. Has that not been one of the elements that contributes to her strong sense of commitment? Adela explains that "promises are promises," so she kept, fulfilled, the "thousands of promises" she made to God in time of trouble. Often it has been said that people like her feel they can buy God's favor. Is it not instead a matter of the reciprocity of a relationship? God did for her, so she does for God by keeping her promises. Marta used to promise thousands of ejaculations, and she could not get out of them lightly. She needed the absolution of a priest. She stopped saying the Girl Scouts' prayer because she could not live it out. Is this not consistent with her sense that Christianity is not just going to church, empty gestures, but the way she lives her life? This parallels Inez's sense that she is involved with the church because she feels it is part of her life.

Lupe does not use the word *promesas* at all. However, this concept was present in her life, but she refers to it as "my mission." She explains it this way.

"The economy at home was very bad, very bad; so when I was fourteen I made a very big decision. I decided that I was going to go to school, study very hard . . . and as soon as I graduated, I was going to start working. Nobody told me, but somehow I decided this, I called it my mission. I wanted my brothers to go to college, and there was no way they were going to go unless I worked. I knew I could do it because I could be a secretary, and I had read that the career of secretary can launch you into anything else. My whole life, that was what I was going to do with my whole life. And I felt real good about it. . . . When I was thirty years old, my youngest sister graduated from college and a week later got married. And then, my mission was complete. . . . And all my life up to then had been my mission. I was working, and I was very lucky to have real good jobs and doing very challenging work, and I was really happy with what I was doing, but the work was only meant to make it possible for me to meet the goal that was my mission. Now that my mission was completed, what was I going to do? It felt very weird."

María never spoke of *promesas*, but her way of dealing with Mary and the saints so they will intercede for her with God and Jesus comes from the same understanding on which making *promesas* are based. It is the same reason why *promesas* are made.

Margarita talked not about the promises she had made but about the promises she says the Virgin Mary has made about Cuba and the Cubans. Mary is as bound as other human persons by the promises she has made. So there is no doubt in Margarita's mind that Mary will have to keep those promises even if it takes a long time.

Sentir, sentimiento

Inez uses this word repeatedly to indicate how her beliefs and what is important to her have to be more than an intellectual exercise or an external compliance. For her, God "is like a *sentimiento*. . . ." Adela has never doubted God. "Any moment, wherever I am, I *siento* his presence." Marta insists that there might be a difference between what she was taught and what she feels; the important thing for her, especially in these difficult times when she is questioning everything, is how she feels and what makes sense to her. Though Marta used the word *feel* in English, she made it a special word by the emphasis she gave it each and every time she used it and the gestures that accompanied the word.

Lupe uses the word *sentir* or its English equivalent much less than the other women. But it comes into play when she is talking of something very important to her. For example, in what was just quoted from her sharing about her decision to make her mission in life to provide the economic resources for her brothers and sisters to go to school, she says, "And I felt real good about it." Then, in talking about one of her most basic beliefs in her day-to-day life, she says, "I feel very connected. . . . I consider myself a part of a lot of people, particularly women; part of many women who went before me, like my grandmother . . . Christian men and women, but mostly I feel a part of many women who came before me. I feel *muy fuerte* [very strong] because I am a part of a lot of women. But, at the same time, I feel very sad, very sad, very alone and very resentful, and I cry a lot because how dare the world not understand the importance of people, of the future, of what I have to do." Notice that when talking about the pride her father has about the work he has done, Lupe does not say, "It *is* an honor for my father to be an unskilled laborer." Instead she says, "He *felt* honored."

María brightens up, and her voice becomes light when she tells us how at this point in her life, she *feels* "fully satisfied." When out of a field of fifty-seven persons, she was one of the nine who won a seat in the school board, "I felt very proud," she says. And when she speaks about God and mentions how at times it seems to her that all the doors are closing, then it is that "I feel something which to me is like a voice . . . that tells me that I can do it."

Olivia does not use the word *sentir* very much. It is all the more important, therefore, to notice that she uses it when talking about her relationship with God. "I *siento* such peace, such happiness when I *siento* his presence in me. You know how when a child hurts his hand and the mother kisses the little hand, the child *se siente* all better? That's the way I *siento* when I talk with him. I *siento* like a little child who goes to him, and by the time I finish talking to him, I know that things are already better."

Margarita uses *sentir* in the way that expresses perhaps the most intensity. She speaks of what great emotion she felt when she participated in the processions in Cuba. This feeling was such an intense reality that even today she gets a physical reaction thinking about it.

All the women pointed emphatically to their hearts when using the word. Is not all this indicative of how very intimately they relate to the divine? What makes sense to them regarding God is that the divine is with them, intimately with them, so *sentir*, which they consider more intimate and a more rounded, complete sense than *knowing*, is what they use.

Iglesia and/or Sacerdote

Iglesia and/or *sacerdote* are words used repeatedly. They are seen as the opposite or, at best, different from, religion, faith, God. Inez says, "I resemble my grandparents a little because they had a lot of faith. It was not a faith based on the *iglesia* [church]. . . . My grandparents did not go to mass, and I go when I have to go, but if

I am very tired or have something else to do, I do not go. The rules of the church did not matter much to them, and neither do they to me. I took in a lot of what today they call popular religiosity." For Adela it has been decided once and for all: she will not go to confession to a *sacerdote* [priest], and she does not like to go to church because she feels their preaching is hypocritical. Therefore, she practices her religion with her children in her home. Marta does not consider that going to church gives her anymore the "spiritual uplift" that it used to give her. So she sees herself as being religious when she takes care of her home and when she shares a Sunday with the family on a boat outing.

Lupe is very connected to church. But what she means by church, the church that is really important to her, is the community—the coming together of the people in her parish and the functions the people organize, direct, and implement. Lupe has been, in her own words, "always very active in the church." She sees her participation as an attempt to live out there what she had learned about religion at home. It is interesting that, though she talked repeatedly about working in her parish, she never mentioned that she has learned anything from the church or the priests.

Only in the area of social justice has she been influenced by church teaching. "For the first time what for me was church and what I did there had a deeper meaning because of the teachings of the Vatican II Council. The Council had just ended, and the message that we were getting was that the Christian needed to be out in the world. And it was around the time when the war on poverty was in its heyday and all those monies started coming for grassroots people to do their own thing, so it was kind of like the church and social issues got together in a real neat way. . . . I took the job I have with this company because I, as a woman, took seriously what her church taught her. . . . There are a lot of things that have to be done for the people, for God's people. . . . There are a lot of people I work with that minimize the value of what I am and what I do. . . . What I think is important because it is what I hear from all the people who come to me. I feel very strongly about the church's responsibility in the area of the prophetic. That is what this church needs to do. The Catholic church needs to be about changing the world to liberate people. To liberate people—that is what the church needs to do."

Lupe connects so strongly with the social teaching of the church because it elucidates as well as perhaps inspires what she feels she needs to do in her life. Again, talking about why she took her job, which brings her in contact with so many needy people and which is so difficult because of the advocacy component, Lupe says, "I really felt it was very much part of what I wanted to do: which was to live my faith out there, to be a Christian everywhere." Because of this, what she likes most in herself is whatever helps her to do her job well. "I like me; I like myself very much when I sit in the midst of a crowded church, when the people come to pray and light candles to Nuestra Señora de Los Lagos, and I get so much from watching the people. And I like me when I am patient, loving, understanding in the face of my enemies, of people who oppose me and what I want to do."

For María the church organizations provide a way of helping her community, of exercising her leadership in the community. There is little or no difference between the reason why she became involved in politics and the reason why she is involved in church groups. She takes from the church what can be life-giving for her. She is very self-assured and does not depend on priest or church to tell her what is right. This becomes very obvious when she relates the following.

"I had my first child when I was eighteen years old, and when I was thirty-six I already had twelve. And the doctors fought a lot with me when I wanted to have an operation [to have her tubes tied]. They said that I was very young, and I was very strong and healthy. I had to beg and cry. At that time there was no pill, and my husband did not believe in trying not to have children, so I would have had twenty-four children if I had listened to them.

"I had all the children that God gave me up to then, and it was still not enough for the priest. I thought that by the time I missed my period, the child in me was fully formed, so I never had an abortion; beside the fact that it was illegal. I would take dark beer with avocado or with castor oil to abort. I would do it at the beginning of finding out that I was pregnant. It did not have any effect on me. The moment came when it was just too much work for me. Then, after the operation when I went to confession, the priest slammed the door of the confessional in my face. I couldn't believe it. I had twelve children and was endangering my health. The priest said to me, "Where does the butcher get the right to feel that he could make that decision?" But, in the end, I do not know what gave me the strength to say in my heart, without words, to the priest, "Look, I do not need you to give me absolution. I fulfilled my duty before God and my country and everything else." I kept on receiving communion.

Some of the women in Olivia's group were complaining about different priests with whom they had very negative experiences. Olivia did not join that conversation except to say about the priests, "They are also human." Her only other comment about a church official was about the permanent deacon who was supposed to supervise her and her husband in the Ministry Program. She felt he did not help them at all and let him know very clearly that he had greatly contributed to their dropping out of the program, but that did not mean she would not be involved in the ministry of God.

Margarita describes herself as someone who always has spent a lot of time in the church. Though she does speak of a few priests and nuns, what fascinates her is her own participation in church functions. Her active role in choirs and processions, in being a connection between her neighborhood and the priest—this is what is fulfilling for her. This is made clear by the fact that she will participate in activities organized not only by her own church, but also by the church of her different friends. Church for her is a set of programs; her deep sense of religion is connected with those programs, and she delights in keeping active in them.

The themes highlighted here begin to make explicit some of the theological implications of the religious understandings of Hispanic Women. These understandings seem to question any and all theologizing of God as totally other—a never changing God. They negate any dualistic understanding of the human person: for Hispanic

Women to feel, to understand, to believe is all one same thing. Hispanic Women have a very deep sense of being the church; for them the clergy is not in any way more religious than they are, or better members of the church than they are. All of these implications and others that can be drawn from the religious understandings of Hispanic Women should be placed at the center of any discussion regarding the role of religion and the church in the Hispanic community.

Significado de «divinidad» para las Mujeres Hispanas

Este capítulo cita a siete Mujeres Hispanas—Inez, Lupe, María, Marta, Adela, Olivia, y Margarita. Lo que estas Mujeres Hispanas han compartido con nosotras debe de ser el punto de partida de toda discusión acerca del papel de la iglesia y la religión en la comunidad Hispana. Sus puntos de vista contradicen toda teología que proclame a Dios como immutable o totalmente ajeno o separado de este mundo.

Promesas.

A Inez la criaron sus abuelos. El abuelo le había prometido a la Virgen del Carmen una vela prendida todas las noches para que ella los protegiera de tormentas. Inez relata como la ha influenciado la fidelidad de su abuelo a su promesa. Adela explica que «promesas son promesas»; es por eso que ella siempre ha cumplido «las miles de promesas» que le ha hecho a Dios en momentos difíciles. Marta le prometía a Dios miles de jaculatorias y sabía que tenía que cumplirlas. Cuando prometía más de lo que podía cumplir, no se podía salir de su obligación fácilmente, y no le quedaba más remedio que ir a pedir la absolución a un sacerdote. Lupe no empleó la palabra *promesa*, pero su sentido de que tenía una misión que cumplir en la vida es igual que el sentido que expresan las promesas—un compromiso, un pacto con Dios y los santos con quienes se puede tratar de igual a igual. Este sentido se revela en la costumbre que tiene María de hablarle continuamente a los santos para que aboguen con Dios por ella. Y Margarita indica claramente como tanto Dios y los santos como los humanos participan plenamente en el mundo de las promesas. Ella habla no de promesas que ha hecho sino de la promesa que según ella la Virgen de La Caridad del Cobre ha hecho de salvar a Cuba: «Puede ser que lleve varias generaciones, ya que tenemos que pagar por nuestros pecados. Pero la Virgen cumplirá su promesa.»

Sentir, sentimiento.

Inez usa estas palabras repetidamente para indicar que sus creencias son más que una afirmación intelectual. «Dios es como un sentimiento», dice Inez. Adela nunca ha dudado de la existencia de Dios porque ella siempre ha sentido su presencia. Marta insiste en que puede ser que haya diferencia entre lo que le enseñaron y lo que siente: lo importante para ella, especialmente ahora que pasa por momentos difíciles, es lo que siente y lo que tiene sentido. Lupe usa poco la palabra *sentir* pero sí la usa al referirse a eventos de mucha importancia en su vida. Cuenta como cuando decidió ser fiel a su misión, «Me sentí muy bien sobre lo que decidí». Y hablando de una creencia muy importante que le da fuerzas para la lucha diaria, Lupe dice, «Yo me siento como parte de muchas mujeres que han vivido antes que yo; me siento muy fuerte porque soy parte de muchas mujeres». María se siente muy satisfecha de su vida. A los sesenta y tres años ha logrado ser una mujer activa como madre, como miembro de la comunidad eclesiástica, y también en el campo de la política. En momentos difíciles, «Siento algo que es como una voz . . . que me dice que sí puedo hacerlo». Olivia usó *sentir* en una sola instancia: «Siento tal paz, tal felicidad cuando siento su presencia. ¿Sabes cómo cuando uno es pequeño y se lastima y la mamá le besa la manita y uno se siento curado? Esa es la forma en que yo me siento cuando hablo con Dios. Me siento como una niña que se acerca a Dios y para cuando termino de conversar con él, sé que ya las cosas van mejor». Margarita cuenta que cuando recuerda las procesiones de Semana Santa en Cuba, «Siento tal emoción que todavía me erizo». El que los sentimientos sean parte integral de las experiencias y creencias religiosas de estas mujeres, ¿no indica acaso lo muy íntima que es su relación con Dios?

Iglesia, sacerdote, cura.

Las mujeres usaron estas palabras repetidamente. Pero en general estas palabras son lo opuesto, o por lo menos algo muy distinto de lo que ellas entienden por religión, fe, Dios. Inez, Lupe, y María participan mucho en sus parroquias, pero para ellas la iglesia es la comunidad. Las tres han tenido experiencias negativas con la iglesia institucional. Inez aprendió de su abuela y su abuelo a no ponerle mucha atención a las reglas de la iglesia. Lupe desde pequeña aprendió que lo importante para su fe no era lo que sucedía en la iglesia, sino lo que aprendía y vivía en su casa. Cuando María tenía treinta y seis años, después de tener doce hijos, decidió hacerse una operación y ligarse los tubos. Cuando fue a confesarse el sacerdote le cerró la puerta en la cara. «Yo no sé qué es lo que me dió la fortaleza de decirme a mí misma, ‹Yo no necesito absolución. Yo cumplo con mi obligación a los ojos de Dios . . . .› Y siempre he seguido yendo a comulgar».

Adela y Marta van muy poco a la iglesia. Adela reza en su casa pero «no, nunca me iré a confesar con un cura». Y a Marta la iglesia ha dejado de ayudarla a sentirse mejor. Ella cree que cumple con sus obligaciones religiosas al compartir el domingo con su familia. Olivia va a la iglesia pero es su propio desarrollo y su relación personal con Dios lo que es importante. Margarita siempre ha ido mucho a la iglesia, y cuando era chiquita quería ser monja. Pero su compromiso no es con la iglesia sino con Dios—un Dios a quien encuentra en diferentes iglesias.

Chapter 3

SOURCE OF HISPANIC WOMEN'S LIBERATION THEOLOGY

The source of Hispanic Women's Liberation Theology is the lived experience of Hispanic Women. Their theology is a critical reflection on their own lived experience. To reach a better understanding of it, their experience can be analyzed from three perspectives: existential, religious, and cultural. These three perspectives are inseparable, informing each other, an intrinsic part of each other. To talk about them separately is but a heuristic device used to make clear specific elements of Hispanic Women's experience.

Existential Perspective

The existential perspective refers to the main preoccupation of Hispanic Women today: survival—survival as a physical reality as well as a cultural one. Survival for Hispanic Women is not a reality that each one can assure just for herself. The survival of Hispanic Women is intrinsically linked with the survival of their community and, in a special way, with the survival of the children of the community. Their hopes, their dreams, their visions, their hard work—all are often for the sake of the children.

Survival for Hispanic Women means a constant struggle against "anthropological poverty," a term used to refer to the kind of oppression that goes beyond material poverty. The anthropological poverty of Hispanic Women threatens to despoil them of their very being. Being or not being is what survival is all about. Hispanic Women are concerned with whatever can threaten or save them—their very being. For Hispanic Women, "being" designates existence in time and space; it means physical survival, and it means cultural survival, which depends to a great extent on self-determination and self-identity.[1] Survival starts with sustaining the physical life, but it does not end there; being or not being also has to do with the social dimension of life. Hispanic Women need bread, but they also need to celebrate. Today they need a roof over their heads, but they also need to have possibilities of a better future for themselves and their children.

The struggle of Hispanic Women for survival is always a struggle against sexism and against ethnic prejudice. For the majority of Hispanic Women, the struggle is also one against poverty, against classism. Starting with Hispanic Women's personal experience, Hispanic Women's Liberation Theology seeks to draw connections between these struggles and "political generalities" about the oppression they suffer. Reflecting on their own experience, Hispanic Women see the connections between their everyday lives and the social institutions that oppress them and influence them. They see the concrete way in which classism, ethnic prejudice/racism, and sexism form a network of prejudices that victimizes them. Hispanic Women's daily lives make them aware of the way the personal and the political are interconnected. As they reflect on their lives and on the personal changes that the struggle for survival requires of them, they come to understand that "changed consciousness and changed definitions of the self can only occur in conjunction with a restructuring of the social relations," both at the societal and personal level in which each one of them is involved.[2]

It is the urgency of their struggle, the absolute need for survival, that leads Hispanic Women to action, to be concerned with praxis. This necessarily means that Hispanic Women's Liberation Theology has to be preoccupied not with orthodoxy—correct belief—but with orthopraxis—"the importance of concrete behavior, of deeds, of action, of praxis. . . ."[3] Hispanic Women are concerned with the kind of behavior, the kind of action, that helps them with the struggle. Therefore, they value religious understandings and beliefs insofar as these encourage and sustain action that helps them survive. Whether these religious understandings and beliefs are sanctioned by the "proper" church authorities is irrelevant to Hispanic Women.

While Hispanic Women share gender and cultural understandings, there are significant differences among them in economics, social placement, education—what is referred to as "class" or "strata." Hispanic Women's Liberation Theology uses the term *strata* because some factors usually not included in the Anglo concept of class are very important and play a major role in determining to which strata any given person might belong. For example, the longer a family has been a member of a given community, the higher the strata to which the members of the family belong; if the family has been among the founders of the town, parish, or organization, the strata of its members is high, regardless of present economic status. Contributing to the strata of a person are her *comadres* and *compadres*—nonblood relatives who enter the family by being sponsors of the children at baptism or by being sponsors and, therefore, advocates of the family because of a wide variety of reasons. It must be understood that these factors must be taken into consideration when it comes to ascertaining the access to privilege and control over their lives that Hispanic Women have within Hispanic circles. Most of these factors are, however, nonoperative in the dealings of Hispanic Women with society at large.

Though the majority of Hispanic Women belong either to the working strata or to the poverty level, a group belonging to the middle strata of society at large is now of sufficient size to be noticed. The majority of those belonging to the middle strata are Cubans; however, increasing numbers of Mexican Americans are part of the middle strata; Puerto Ricans comprise the smallest number of middle strata Hispanic Women.

Middle strata Hispanic Women might have "only their labor power to sell," which, strictly speaking, would make them members of the working strata. But, though the actual money they have might be limited, middle strata women have access to privilege and can control their lives to a greater extent; in other words, survival for them is a strong possibility.[4] However, even for middle strata Hispanic Women, this possibility of survival is often threatened by the ethnic prejudice they suffer. They are keenly aware that maintenance of their membership in the middle strata often depends on their ability and/or willingness to conform to Anglo culture. They also realize that, together with Anglo women, they are often "a man away from welfare"—that their economic status and prestige is, in great part, determined by whose daughters, sisters, wives, they are.

Though the struggle for physical survival is not a daily factor in the lives of middle strata Hispanic Women, survival is still their main preoccupation. Survival for them is cultural and psychological. It has to do with questions of self-definition and self-determination. Survival for a middle strata Hispanic Woman is related to the difficult task of living in a culture that is not her own; it comes down repeatedly to choosing between faithfulness to self or, at the risk of losing cultural values and identity, buying into the dominant culture in order to maintain her status.

Religious Perspective

Analyzing the religious perspective of experience leads once again to the affirmation that the source of Hispanic Women's Liberation Theology is the lived experience of Hispanic Women. Such an affirmation stands in contrast to what other theologies claim.

Paul Tillich, for example, like the vast majority of theologians, claims that the Bible "is the basic source of systematic theology." "Denominational tradition" is another source of theology for Tillich. In spite of the fact that Tillich considers theology of culture central to systematic theology, for him human experience is not a source but rather "the medium through which the sources 'speak' . . . through which [they are] receive[d]. . . . "[5]

For Gustavo Gutiérrez, one of the leading Latin American liberation theologians, "Theology must be man's [sic] critical reflection on himself [sic], on his [sic] own basic principles . . . a critical theory worked out in the light of the Word accepted in faith and inspired by a practical purpose." What Gutiérrez proposes is a rereading of the gospel using a hermeneutics of suspicion. The source of theology for him is a combination of the Word and the experience of oppression of the poor. The end product is to be a "political hermeneutics of the gospel."[6]

Elisabeth Schüssler Fiorenza proposes a feminist critical hermeneutics that claims not only the "contemporary community of women struggling for liberation as its locus of revelation, it also must reclaim its foresisters as victims *and* subjects participating in patriarchal culture." She boldly affirms that "biblical revelation and truth are given only in those texts and interpretative models that transcend critically their patriarchal frameworks and allow for a vision of Christian women as historical and theological subjects and actors." She states that "the criterion of appropriateness for biblical interpretation and evaluation of biblical authority claims" is whether it is liberating for women and other oppressed people now.[7] Schüssler Fiorenza is thus preoccupied with finding an appropriate way of dealing with the biblical text. The source for her theology is a combination of the Bible and the personal and political struggle of women for liberation.

Why does Hispanic Women's Liberation Theology claim the lived experience of Hispanic Women as its source? First of all, Hispanic Women as persons who are "vitally engaged in historical realities with specific times and places,"[8] and who concern themselves with and reflect on matters of ultimate concern. This reflection includes religious considerations, which form "a system of symbols which acts to establish powerful, pervasive, and long-lasting moods and motivations in . . . [them] by formulating conceptions of general order of existence and clothing these conceptions with such an aura of factuality that the moods and motivations seem uniquely realistic."[9] Many of these powerful symbols arise out of a certain kind of "official" Christian tradition in which the Bible is claimed to be, but is not, central.[10] They also arise out of the African traditions brought to Latin America by the slaves, and the Amerindian traditions bequeathed by the great Aztec, Maya, and Inca civilizations, as well as other Amerindian cultures such as Taíno, Siboney, Caribe, Araucano, and others.

Religion is central in the lives of Hispanic Women. It is precisely their religion, their deep sense of an existential interconnection between themselves and the divine, that provides the "moods and motivations" for their struggle for survival. In other words, the religious dimension in their lives constitutes a "revolutionary urge." It is precisely the struggle for survival that defines the essence of religion for Hispanic Women.[11]

The term that has been used to speak about the religion of Hispanic Women, about their connection with the divine, is *Christianity*. In reality the Christianity of Hispanic Women does not necessarily have the church as its main point of reference. It is a Christianity of a very specific variety due in part to its history in the countries in which Hispanic Women have their ethnic roots.

Christianity came to Latin America at the time of the *conquista*. It came not only, or even primarily, in the form of an organized religion, but as an intrinsic part of the conquering culture. The term *conquista* denotes not just a political conquest, but rather a total conquest in which even the religious world of the conquered suffered total devastation. What took place was indeed a process of acculturation during which the culture of the conqueror was imposed unilaterally on the conquered people. Christianity as an intrinsic element of that culture was not only imposed but also played a very important role as moral justifier in the whole process of the *conquista*. Real enculturation—"the process of making personal the traditional culture of the society," i.e., the society of the *conquistadores*—did not take place because education was not made available to the vast majority of the population. Instead what resulted was a "culturization" of Christianity; Christianity became culture; it has become a cultural expression.[12] But this cultural expression called Christianity is made up of Amerindian and African beliefs and practices as well as Christian ones.

The Christianity of Latin America and that of Hispanics in the United States—very similar but not identical varieties of Christian ity—have two distinctive elements that are not always able to be separated. They are "official" Christian tradition, and African and Amerindian beliefs and traditions. How does Hispanic Women's Liberation Theology deal with these two religious strands? It deals with them the same way Hispanic Women do. It takes from each of them what is life giving, what is important for the struggle for survival, and leaves aside what is not relevant or is harmful.[13]

Hispanic Women's Liberation Theology and "Official" Christianity

"Official" Christianity is comprised of "those prescribed beliefs and norms of an institution [in a special way but not exclusively of the Catholic church] promulgated and monitored by a group of religious specialists." Because of historical development within Christianity in general and the Catholic church in particular, in Latin America the biblical basis of the "prescribed beliefs and norms" was/is not taught or emphasized. This has resulted in a variety of Christianity that uses the Bible in a very limited way, emphasizing the traditions and commandments of the church more than the scriptural basis of Christianity.[14]

It is not surprising, therefore, that in the lives of Hispanic Women the Bible does not play a prominent role. They do not read the Bible and know only popularized versions of biblical stories—versions Hispanic Women create to make a point but that often distort or imaginatively interpret the original versions.[15] Their Christianity is informed by Christian tradition and practice rather than by the Bible. So, for example, Hispanic Women will pray the rosary rather than read the Bible, and not necessarily because they cannot read or read poorly; they will be sure to be on time for a procession but are not concerned about arriving at a church service in time to listen to Scripture readings. Accordingly, even though Hispanic Women's Liberation Theology relates to the Bible peripherally, it does not reject it in its totality. Biblical revelation and truth are not negated, but they are not given much attention, simply because they are not part of the daily experience of Hispanic Women.

Hispanic Women's Liberation Theology and Popular Religiosity

The "official" church has understood popular religiosity as "those patterns of behavior and belief that somehow escape the control of institutional specialists, existing alongside (and sometimes despite) the effort at control of these specialists."[16]

Popular religiosity is part of the source of Hispanic Women's Liberation Theology to the extent that, and insofar as, popular religiosity is an intrinsic part of the daily lives of Hispanic Women. Hispanic Women's Liberation Theology understands popular religiosity as a rich tradition of religious beliefs and practices that fuses Christian, Amerindian, and African religious traditions and is the most operative "system of symbols" used by Hispanic Women in establishing "powerful, pervasive, and long-lasting moods and motivations"[17] in their lives.

Some of the African and Amerindian elements, which "official" Christianity has neglected or rejected, but which are very important in popular religiosity, could well offer needed correctives to some of the religious understandings of "official" Christianity. For example, Our Lady of Regla, a title of Mary sanctioned by "official" Catholicism in Cuba, is often identified in popular religiosity with Yemaya, the Goddess of the Sea in the Lucumi religion, one of the African religions brought to Cuba by the African slaves.

Yemaya is strong, powerful and serious mother of the rest of the deities, goddess of fertility but not of love. In spite of her wisdom and prudence, sometimes Yemaya is passionate and sensual. . . .[18]

If "official" Christianity would accept passion and sensuality as attributes of Mary, would this not help it to have a much more realistic understanding of the morality of sexuality?

Popular religiosity has often been a source of embarrassment for "official" Christianity. What the "official" church has done, therefore, is either denounce it and work actively against it or look for ways of purifying it, of "baptizing" it into Christianity—accepting only those elements that can be Christianized.[19] Hispanic Women's Liberation Theology sees this as an imperialistic approach that refuses to recognize and accept as true, good, and life giving any and all religious understandings and practices that do not directly relate to their understanding and interpretation of the gospel, that do not have Christ as center, model, and norm.[20] Hispanic Women's Liberation Theology takes exception to such refusal because it does violence to a valid understanding of Jesus as portrayed in Scripture: Jesus clearly indicated that his mission was not to point at himself, but rather to point out the way to God.

Such imperialism is also anticultural and anti-Hispanic for two reasons. First, a noticeable number of Hispanic Women either do not believe that Jesus was divine, or they do not consider him or his divinity something relevant in their lives.[21] Second, Hispanic Women's religious understandings and beliefs, with African, Amerindian, and Christian elements, constitute an intrinsic part of Hispanic culture. Therefore, to reject, attempt to eliminate, and/or radically change the African and Amerindian elements is to do violence to the Hispanic culture.

Hispanic Women's Christianity is indeed a mixture, a fusion of different religious strands. In this regard Hispanic Women's Liberation Theology follows in the footsteps of "official" Christianity, which from its early history has been syncretistic. The Greco-Roman world of ideas and understandings, plus the understandings of what Jesus preached, came together—fused—to form Christianity. For example, Christmas is celebrated at the time of the year when pagan sun feasts used to take place; pagan buildings such as the Pantheon were turned into churches; civil offices and garb became religious offices and liturgical garb; Greek philosophical concepts of substance and form became the language used to talk about the Eucharist. Once this syncretism became official, it was used as the orthodox norm, which excluded and excludes other syncretisms.

But such an exclusion does not obliterate syncretism from the religion of Hispanic Women. Who is Our Lady of Guadalupe? Is she the Mother of Jesus? Or is she Tonantzin, the Aztec goddess, Mother of the Gods on whose pilgrimage site, the hill of Tepeyac, Our Lady of Guadalupe appeared?[22] In their hearts, if not openly, Cubans who pray to St. Barbara are very often identifying her, directly or indirectly, with Chango, the Yoruban God of Thunder. It is irrelevant to them that the hierarchy of the church has indicated the story of St. Barbara is a legend and that most probably such a person never existed. The churches might have removed her statues, but she continues to be one of the most popular saints among Cubans.

The history of Christianity shows that orthodox objections to syncretism have to do not with the purity of faith, but with who has the right to determine what is to be considered normative and official. For the articulation of religious understandings, beliefs, and practices to be an act of liberation, it has to be an act of self-determination and not an attempt to comply with what the "official" church says. This is why Hispanic Women do not shrink from claiming that the fusion of Christian, Amerindian, and African religious strands operative in their lives is good and life giving.

But, because Scripture *per se* is not an intrinsic element of the source of Hispanic Women's Liberation Theology, and, therefore, christological questions are peripheral, is this theology Christian theology? And, if a significant number of Hispanic Women do not believe in the divinity of Jesus or think it is irrelevant, are they Christians? The answer to both of these questions is affirmative for the following reasons.

- The self-definition of a vast number of persons is an intrinsic element of reality. The overwhelming majority of Hispanic Women see themselves, understand themselves as, and claim to be Christians. The majority consider themselves Catholics even if they go to other churches.
- The religious understandings operative in Hispanic Women's lives use Western Christianity as the basic paradigm for expressing their religious moods and motivations.[23]

- Though there are indeed differences, the basic understandings of Hispanic Women's popular religiosity are not antithetical to the core of the gospel message: justice and love.
- The Christian practices that are influential and part of popular religiosity are themselves mostly formed by the intermingling of Christianity and other religious traditions of the past— intermingling that was the popular religiosity of peoples of ages past.

Cultural Perspective

The survival of Hispanic Women is directly related to the fate of Hispanic culture.[24] This is why Hispanic culture is one of the elements of Hispanic Women's Liberation Theology. A second reason is that, adapting the description of one of the models suggested by H. Richard Niebuhr regarding the relationship between Christ and culture, Hispanic Women feel no great tension between their religion and the world, the workings of the divine and human effort, the religious motivation for action and the motivation of justice for the Hispanic community. On the one hand, they see their culture through "Christianity"; on the other hand, they understand "Christianity" through culture, selecting from it such points as seem most relevant to their struggle as Hispanic Women.[25] This is also one of the reasons why Hispanic Women's Liberation Theology claims to be cultural theology.

Following Niebuhr's lead, one can indeed say that Hispanic culture and Hispanic Women's Liberation Theology live in symbiosis[26]—they live in close relationship, each benefiting from such an association. Hispanic Women's Liberation Theology is a praxis that happens within the Hispanic culture, for the articulation of cultural religious understandings is intrinsic to the self-understanding and self-definition of this culture. It is, therefore, cultural theology because it is done within the Hispanic culture. Hispanic Women's Liberation Theology is a praxis expressed from within the culture, of revelation found in the "symbolic system of meanings, values and norms of [the] culture."[27] Yet the relationship of Hispanic Women's Liberation Theology to culture has another important aspect. While maintaining its symbiotic relationship with culture, Hispanic Women's Liberation Theology also critiques culture. Using Hispanic Women's struggle for survival as its critical lens, it critiques culture from within. It is precisely this critical stance based on the lived experience of Hispanic Women that is both a beginning and one of the elements of Hispanic Women's culture.

What understandings of culture are operative in Hispanic Women's Liberation Theology? First of all, culture is not a betterment of human nature but a human condition that has developed through history. Human nature does not exist in a pure form, "nor has there existed in history a state of nature, counterposed to a state of culture . . . ." Culture is a social reality because it has to do not only with the individual person but also with a particular social group. Culture has to do with patterns of thoughts, feelings, and behavior of a person learned from the human group in which the individual grows —patterns of relationships and social structures that the group uses to organize itself.[28]

Cultures have not only an "organic structure," but also a "vivifying element, the 'soul' of each culture, which 'shapes' in a particular way each one of them." To a large extent the soul, the vivifying element, of Hispanic Women's culture is the religious dimension. It is around and in relation to the religious dimension that the motivations of this culture are established. All the elements of Hispanic Women's culture are united, "the cultural values are ordered and the aspirations and ideals of [the] culture are centered" around religious understanding and beliefs.[29]

Furthermore, because the religious dimension is the most important structuring factor of Hispanic Women's culture, the religious institutions—and these go far beyond what is understood by church—are an integral part of it, "receiving their full cultural significance in the interior of the structure of culture and in the light of its total configuration."[30]

Hispanic Women's culture is not a closed system but an open one in two directions: inwardly toward the Hispanic Woman who through culture is historically realized, in it she lives and expresses herself. But at the same time, [if she is involved in the struggle for liberation] she always transcends it and is the source of constant innovation, transformation, and self-betterment; in the second place, culture is a totality open to the exteriorness of other cultures not only through the understanding and dialogue that the human persons establish with other cultures, past and present, but also through the relationship between cultural alienation (mainly understood here as false identification with the essence of the other) and domination.[31]

As a culture that lives within another culture, Hispanic Women's culture constantly becomes "implicitly or explicitly meaningful to the participants . . . during communication across some kind of social boundary. . . . Hispanic Women's culture can best be perceived and understood in the day-to-day experience and history of Hispanic Women, which together shape in them "a certain fundamental attitude . . . a way of comprehending and valuing themselves, others and nature, a comprehension which determines the relationship of these three."[32]

"Fundamental attitude" in this context is not to be understood as a vision or philosophy. Fundamental attitude refers to the "soul" of a culture, which precedes philosophy. Fundamental attitude is not constructed by "reflection but is unveiled, discovered."[33] The "soul" of Hispanic Women's culture, as already stated, is the religious dimension in Hispanic Women's lives.

Hispanic Women's culture is being birthed right here and now. As stated earlier, Hispanic Women bring together three different cultural strands: Spanish, Amerindian, and African. The cultures of the three main Hispanic groups in the United States—Cubans, Mexican Americans, and Puerto Ricans—have been influenced by two or three of these strands, but the importance given to each strand and the appropriation of each of them have differed according to the geographical, historical, and political conditions of each of these groups. Here in the United States the three groups come together, and new cultural patterns begin to emerge according to the reality Hispanic Women face. Hispanic Women's culture is in the process of becoming. The main reason why this is happening now is that the need for both economical and cultural survival has led Hispanic Women to begin to understand themselves as one, to find similarities among themselves and capitalize on them; to see differences not as dangerous and divisive, but as an enriching factor.

Hispanic Women's culture begins to exist because the creation of "the systems of symbols that express and transmit the experiences, accumulated knowledge, the beliefs and values"[34] of Hispanic Women has started. Furthermore, Hispanic Women's culture is beginning to be able to provide for Hispanic Women a way of mediating their activity to the rest of the world; it is beginning to form social structures of relationships that respond to the way Hispanic Women, individually and as a group, deal with their reality. The importance of Hispanic Women's Liberation Theology lies in its being an intrinsic element in the process of creating a Hispanic Women's culture and an articulation of the new reality being birthed.[35]

Fuente de «Teología de la liberación de la Mujer Hispana»

La fuente de la teología de la liberación de la Mujer Hispana es la experiencia vivida por la Mujer Hispana. Esta experiencia se puede analizar desde tres perspectivas: cultural, religiosa, y existencial. Estas tres perspectivas constituyen una misma realidad, ya que son parte intrínseca una de las otras. Si se presentan aquí por separado es sólo como método heurístico para así poder entender mejor los pormenores de dicha experiencia.

Perspectiva existencial

Esta perspectiva tiene que ver con la preocupación principal de las Mujeres Hispanas: su supervivencia y la de sus comunidades. Para sobrevivir hay que luchar constantemente en contra de la pobreza antropológica—pobreza que va más allá de lo material amenazando a la Mujer Hispana al nivel del «ser o no ser» tanto físico como cultural. El «ser o no ser» a nivel cultural depende de la posibilidad que la Mujer Hispana tiene de auto-determinarse y auto-identificarse. Sabiendo que la opresión que sufren es tanto estructural como personal, las Mujeres Hispanas luchan en contra del sexismo, el prejuicio étnico, y el clasismo. La urgencia de la lucha por sobrevivir hace comprender a las Mujeres Hispanas que lo importante es tener una praxis liberativa y no ideas más o menos buenas. Es por eso que esta teología de la liberación de la Mujer Hispana se preocupa más por la ortopraxis que por la ortodoxia.

Los prejuicios étnicos y el sexismo afectan a todas las Mujeres Hispanas, pero existen grandes diferencias entre ellas cuando se habla del clasismo. Aunque la mayoría de las Mujeres Hispanas pertenecen a la clase trabajadora o están por debajo del nivel demarcador de la pobreza, existe un grupo lo suficientemente grande como para ser notado que pertenece a la clase media. Entre éstas el mayor porcentaje es de cubanas; le siguen las mexicano-americanas y las puertorriqueñas. Sin embargo, las Mujeres Hispanas de la clase media no están fuera de peligro, ya que muchas veces su estado económico depende de sus familias. Muchas veces sus posibilidades de sobrevivir son mejores, no por el dinero que tienen, sino por las conexiones que han forjado—conexiones que hacen posible ejercer un poco de control sobre sus propias vidas. Tanto las Mujeres Hispanas de clase media como las de clase trabajadora y las pobres tienen que luchar a nivel sicológico y cultural, escogiendo continuamente entre ser fieles a sí mismas como Hispanas o aceptar la cultura dominante para poder salir adelante.

Perspectiva religiosa

La religión es parte integral de toda cultura y forma «un sistema de símbolos que actúa para establecer disposiciones y motivaciones poderosas, penetrantes y duraderas . . . ya que formula conceptos generales acerca de la vida y reviste estos conceptos con tal aura de veracidad que las disposiciones y motivaciones se convierten en realidades auténticas» (Geertz). La dimensión religiosa es para las Mujeres Hispanas un impulso revolucionario y es, por lo tanto, la lucha por sobrevivir lo que define lo que es esencialmente religioso. Pero la religión de las Mujeres Hispanas es un sincretismo que conjuga el cristianismo con entendimientos y prácticas de las religiones africanas y las amerindias. El cristianismo de la cultura Hispana está basado más en tradiciones y enseñanzas de la iglesia que en la Biblia. La religiosidad popular juega un papel muy importante en la vida de las Mujeres Hispanas y ofrece correctivos que la «religión oficial» no quiere aceptar. Esto resulta en una actitud imperialista y anti-cultural por parte de la «religión oficial» ya que la religiosidad popular es parte integral de la cultura Hispana.

Perspectiva cultural

La supervivencia de la Mujer Hispana depende de la supervivencia de su cultura—razón por la cual la cultura es uno de los elementos de esta teología de la liberación de la Mujer Hispana. Para la Mujer Hispana no existe tensión entre su religión y el mundo, el trabajo divino y el humano, la motivación religiosa y la motivación en favor de la justicia para su comunidad. La cultura Hispana y la clase específica de cristianismo en la cual operan los entendimientos africanos y amerindios viven en simbiosis. Es por esto que esta teología de la liberación de la Mujer Hispana es una praxis dentro de la cultura Hispana que explicita el sistema de significados, valores, y normas religiosas de las Mujeres Hispanas. Esta teología entiende la cultura no como un mejoramiento de la naturaleza humana sino como una condición humana que se ha ido desarrollando a través de la historia. La cultura tiene una estructura orgánica y un alma que le da características propias. El alma de la cultura Hispana es en gran parte la religión—la clase de cristianismo mencionado anteriormente.

La cultura de la Mujer Hispana está en proceso de nacer aquí y hoy. Es una cultura que conjuga las herencias española, africana, y amerindia con la realidad socio-histórica que viven las Mujeres Hispanas hoy en Estados Unidos. Esta teología de la liberación de la Mujer Hispana es un elemento intrínseco en este proceso de dar a luz la cultura de la Mujer Hispana a la vez que es articulación de la realidad que está naciendo.

Chapter 4

HISPANIC WOMEN'S ETHICAL UNDERSTANDINGS

As stated at the very beginning of this book, moral theology or ethics, together with theological themes usually classified under systematics, form a single unit for Hispanic Women's Liberation Theology. To speak of ethics and ethical understandings separate from systematics is, therefore, a heuristic device made necessary by the inability to speak of several things at the same time in an intelligible way.

In its attempts to develop an adequate social ethics, Hispanic Women's Liberation Theology starts by asserting that the individual as a moral agent is "responsible for both interpersonal and social life." This does away with separating the private from the public sphere of morality. Furthermore, Hispanic Women will no longer allow themselves to be confined to the private sphere. They will adamantly insist that, because they are moral agents, they have an active role to play in social transformation.[1] The basis for this is the anthropological understanding that Hispanic Women are *imago Dei*.

An adequate understanding of social ethics for Hispanic Women also has to make explicit from the very beginning the social theories it takes into consideration.[2] When Hispanic Women's Liberation Theology looks at different social theories, the first element it evaluates is whether the social theory being considered is based on the belief, demonstrable in action, that the freedom of the individual is intrinsically linked to the self-determination of the community to which she belongs. The social theory also must propose concretely how the self-determination of the person, who is necessarily a member of the community, will be attained in a way that does not manipulate nor diminish any other person or community.

Second, Hispanic Women's Liberation Theology seeks to redefine power as enablement and creativity rather than control and domination; it also claims that relationality is intrinsic to the human person—the only way there is to participate in who/what is divine.[3] Enablement and relationality act as guides for all ethical activity; "all relationships of domination and subordination—whether between two people or within a system comprised of people—need to be overcome." These understandings of power as enablement and relationality are what shape the struggle for liberation of Hispanic Women—a struggle that seeks not to participate in the present patriarchal oppressive structures, but to bring about a radical change in those structures. The goal is to establish a new order of relationships in which salvation becomes a reality when there is no domination and alienation. The struggle for liberation, a historical reality, becomes the incarnational realization of salvation. Enablement and relationality make present "salvific moments"[4] that make visible the dreams and hopes of Hispanic Women.

Third, due to Hispanic Women's Liberation Theology's "concern with systemic oppression and its focus on praxis, [it has to] provide moral criteria for evaluating relevant public policy. . . ."[5] Such criteria follow a specific form of ethical understanding in which the way Hispanic Women achieve their goal of liberation/survival is an intrinsic part of the goal itself. The struggle for liberation/survival becomes a way of life "in which one sets oneself to do whatever one is trying to do,"[6] rather than an objective outside of one's life acquired through certain means. Hispanic Women achieve survival/liberation when they risk, when they struggle, when they love, when they use their creative power for the good of the community; they do not risk, struggle, and love in order to survive and be liberated. The way of life informed by the struggle for liberation/survival delineates all that Hispanic Women do, including the making of moral judgments.

Because such moral judgments are a personal matter—the personal being grounded in, and depending on, the community—the struggle for liberation has to do not only with commitment by a given Hispanic Woman, but also with her relations with others within her community and with other communities that also struggle for liberation.

Moral judgments also have to take into consideration principles—principles that are not "codifications of past taboos [but] distillations of reflection on how, generally speaking, and apart from very special reasons to the contrary, we have decided that it is best to behave."[7] The principles operative in the moral judgments of Hispanic Women are part of their religious beliefs and understandings—one of the reasons why religion is an intrinsic part of Hispanic Women's struggle for liberation/survival.

Feelings, a human capacity/power of extreme importance in the Hispanic culture, are also intrinsic to the moral criteria of Hispanic Women. The outward expression of feeling is important for the individual Hispanic Woman, and it is also an essential part of her relationship with the community at large. Feelings are indeed "a source of imaginative insight"[8] and a motivation for praxis that goes well beyond any and all reasoning. This is why they have to be understood as intrinsic to principles, to strategies for action—to the struggle for liberation/survival, the way of life of Hispanic Women.

The centrality of struggle in the life of Hispanic Women necessarily makes moral criteria both dialogical and problematic, embracing a variety of concepts that gain predominance, given the situation at hand.[9] The criteria become dialogical when it does not dictate from above but rather enters into dialogue with both what is happening and who it is happening to. This dialogue is precisely what makes the moral criteria problematic. Easy and neat solutions are no longer possible once dialogue makes moral criteria relinquish its authoritarian attitude. The situation at hand is not judged abstractly nor lightly, but it is judged according to the praxis it generates. Again, orthopraxis, not orthodoxy, is what is most important in the formulation and evaluation of Hispanic Women's moral criteria.

Fourth, Hispanic Women's Liberation Theology will continue to critique seriously the sexism, ethnic prejudice, and classism of "official" Christianity. At the same time, Hispanic Women's Liberation Theology will critique the ethnic prejudice and classism it finds in feminism and will also critique the sexism and ethnic/racial prejudices of Latin American Liberation Theology. In other words, Hispanic Women's Liberation Theology will critique the sexism, classism, and ethnic prejudice of all institutions and ideologies because of the way in which they influence and determine the moral life of Hispanic Women.

The verbatim material that follows provides the basis for, and begins to clarify and accomplish, what these four points enunciate. Only when one listens to their whole story can one begin to understand how Hispanic women see themselves, what kind of society they hope for, how they deal with and critique the world in which they live. Since it is impossible to include here their whole stories, what follows are the responses of the same Hispanic Women who spoke about the divine in Chapter 2 to questions dealing specifically with good and evil. The women found it difficult to answer these questions. Several questions were used to help them conceptualize what they were being asked to address: What is the best thing that has happened to you or that you have done? What is the best thing that could happen in our world today? What is the worst experience, the most difficult experience you have had? What is the worst thing in our world today?

The wording of the questions purposefully excluded "religious" language. The authors had great concern that, when dealing with these questions, the women would not verbalize what they really believe, what is really operative in their lives. The concern was not unfounded. Often in surveys conducted by religious groups, Hispanic Women will answer what they think the interviewer expects them to say or what they know to be the church's teaching, even though they do not necessarily believe it.[10] The use of nonreligious language in these questions, therefore, helped to bring to the surface the real moral/ethical understandings of the women. It was also helpful that there was no one present who was in a position of authority in the church. Finally, the trust level was very high among the women who participated; this indeed facilitated open and truthful sharing.

Inez

She answered without any hesitation. "Many important things have happened in my life." When she was asked to think in terms of "good things" instead of "important things," she nodded her head. However, her answer makes it obvious that for her what is good is important. Here is some of what she said:

"One thing is that my grandparents raised me; for me that was very good because it shaped me. The other thing is to have met the woman I call my teacher. Thanks to her I am committed, . . . I am Inez [and Inez said both her first and last names, indicating that she was referring to her whole self]. She gave us a vision of life, not only to me but to twelve of us young women and men. And I think that is the most important thing in the life of any person—to have a vision. Because, even if everything goes wrong, if you have a vision, you will continue *luchando* [struggling] because that vision is something stronger than you. So the prettiest, the most beautiful thing, was to be able to have a person who gave me a vision when I was very young.

"I want to add that I always have the greatest respect [the sense here is that she renders homage to] for Aida Luz [her mentor when she was a teenager] who gave us so much vision. And something that I am always grateful to her for is that she taught us to ask, to raise questions. In Puerto Rico, because of the political situation, they always taught us that we should accept everything. They would speak to us about George Washington, and we had to say, 'Amen.' They spoke to us of Abraham Lincoln, 'Amen.' Because we are a colony. But we could never ask anything. And she taught us to ask. She would say, 'Ask; you were created in the image of God and you can ask, you do not have to accept it all.' "

When it came to speaking about evil, Inez immediately identified it with what is painful. "The most painful thing was when they took me out of Puerto Rico, and they obliged me to come here. When I was eleven years old, my mother said, 'She is going over there.' Yes, the worst was that they took me out of my land, that they devalued what was valuable for me. Like when they laughed when I talked about the animals, when I talked about the fields, and they laughed at me for not speaking English. Even Mom used to say, 'Ah, this one is a *jíbara*.' [This is what people from the Puerto Rican countryside are called. It is used pejoratively to connote lack of education and culture.] . . . . At that time, everything in my life disappeared. My grandmother died, the fields were gone, the animals were no longer there—everything was finished for me because they brought me back to the *país frío* [cold country—here it refers not only to climate but to the lack of nurturing she has found in the United States]. It was as if they took away all my values, they took away everything I was; everything that I was, was taken away from me. Everything in me collapsed. Life ended for me. Many times I thought it would be good to die, or to kill myself. The convent was horrible, but this time was worse because I was demoralized. I think that is why today I am so strong about my culture and about what is mine, what I respected and what I loved—they devalued it; they destroyed me. . . . For me not to value another is a crime. When we believe in ourselves, when the persons who have raised us have told us that we are worth something, then not to love a person for who she is—to devalue her for whatever foolish reasons—that is a crime."

Adela

For Adela, goodness has to do with love. "The best thing is to love one another, for all to love each other. To love, to help, to understand, to watch out for your friends, your family, to do for each other." A discussion arose in the group regarding whether one should use what one has to get ahead, or whether instead it should be shared. Adela's participation in this discussion further illustrates her understanding of love.

Clara: One should first help oneself.

Esther: Yes, so you can accumulate more and then have more to give.

Flor: I think one should better oneself first so you can help others afterwards.

Adela: I don't know, it must be that I think differently; I think that if I in my house have three beds, two heaters, I would give half of what I have.

Esther: But to have three beds, two heaters, you had to work more and save. . . .

Clara: . . . . But I would not give my things, but I would share what I have. . . .

Adela: There are times when things like that happen, and I do not mind not having anything left. If I have ten dollars or one dollar, and I know that is all I have, and I see a person who perhaps needs it more than I do, I give it. I let it go without pain and without anything; I would give it like that and would not mind having nothing left. Maybe I am wrong, but it comes from within me, without saying, "Ay, how am I going to give it?" I know that the next moment is going to bring something else, and up to now, it has always brought twice as much. Because I do not feel that I have too little.

Lola: I have a relative who gives even his boots. He took to my mother's [to live there with her and for her to take care of him] a boy from Puebla—God only knows if he is a good or bad boy.

Enabler: If I say, "First I will get ahead, and then, when I have two, I will give you one," well, I think I will then want both. . . . If I cannot give up one, much less am I going to give up two or more.

Adela: The more they have, the more they want.

For Adela the worst evil has to do with not being a good mother to her children. "For me the worst would be not to give an education to my children. I already lived my life, now it is my turn to form [educate] them. For me it would be very bad if my children would acquire bad habits; it would be a sin because I am the one responsible for them here. It would be a sin for me not to take my children down the right path, so that they would start to get into bad habits; that would be the worst sin I could commit.

"What has hurt me most is the contempt the people here in the United States have for us [Mexicans]. Not all, but there are so many who have hurt us so very much.

"The sickness of my son and the moment he was sick, that is what hurts me."

Question: What do you mean when you say you have lived your life? You still have half of your life—you are only 34!

"My life right now is my children, for me there is no other life, I have given my life to my children. For me, I wish I could better myself so I could do better for them. I do not plan to become stagnant; I am thinking of studying and becoming better, to become better for them. . . . For me, first and above all other plans, my children. I love them so much, I gave them my life."

Marta

Though there is a vast class difference between Adela and Marta, they think along the same lines. For Marta, goodness is also closely connected to her family. "The best thing that has happened to me is my family—having the relationships of my kids, my sister, and my parents. More and more, as life goes on and I see other human beings relating in this life, I value what we have, the ability of all of us to relate to each other. . . . Not many other people are capable of that in life anymore. I used to take it for granted, but now I appreciate it tremendously because what we have is very, very special.

"The worst is disloyalty—that for me is very hard to deal with. I cannot conceive of being disloyal because for me that is the worst. To be loyal is to be true to you, not ever giving up on you. To be disloyal is to give up on you, or letting you down. If you need me, I am going to be there. Loyalty is when I have to choose between you and another person or between you and a wish of mine, and you come out first. That's being loyal. Loyalty to me is very important.

"I do think in terms of loyalty to myself. Whatever I hear or see, if it makes sense to me, I take it in—that is being loyal to myself. My goal in life is to make those around me happy, and I could not make my kids happy if I was not happy. So, at all times, I am very careful of not putting aside my happiness. . . . So it is not sacrifice, sacrifice, sacrifice, because I tend to do that; but that is not good for me. . . . I have to think of myself so that the giving doesn't go overboard, and then I am not happy."

Lupe

Lupe does not need to think. She knows immediately what is the worst thing that has happened to her. "There is lots of bad, but what I think is the worst—well, I think of it as losing my innocence. I had grown up believing that if I did certain things, if I worked hard, everything would turn out fine. My father told me that when one works, one has to give the employer our best. 'If there is nothing to do, pick up a broom and sweep,' he would tell me. And that is the way I was. I was working in an emergency shelter and food pantry, and, because I speak Spanish and a lot of our clients were Hispanics, I did a lot of direct service besides clerical work. I had given myself to my job completely. I had no social life, I did not keep up with friends. The only thing I still did was teach at the parish once a week. Anyway, we got a new boss, and one day, out of the clear blue sky—it was December 22, 1966—I will never forget it, this man called me to the office and told me he was going to sue me for libel because I had been defacing his character, and I had been gossiping and saying he behaved immorally. We all worked in the same room, so everybody was around. And I looked at my coworkers, wondering if anyone was going to stand up for me. And nobody did. And I looked around, and they were all my friends, they were all my friends; we went to picnics, and we talked . . . and everybody just stood there. And I stood there and started crying and yelling, 'It is not true.' And I remember that my legs gave way, and I sank to the floor screaming, screaming as if somebody had killed me. The only person who came to pick me up was Martha—and she was a visitor that day. I barely knew her. What hurt me most was the disillusionment; I had given my all, and it had not mattered. This is the worst thing that has happened to me because of what happened inside me; I gave up expecting that I would be dealt with fairly. . . . I could give my all, and I would still not be treated right."

When it comes to talking about the best thing that has happened to her, Lupe cannot give specifics, though she has a clear idea of what is the best for her. Her answer is quite short in comparison with the lengthy story she shared about the worst experience in her life. "All of us here who work with the people have the best. The best are situations that open me to grow more, to serve more. So, when at thirty I got married, that was so good because I was able to be more by having a deep relationship with another person. I risked; I left my family and even moved away for a short while. I risked everything for the possibility of this relationship."

María

In a quiet but very firm way María shares with the group what has been the very best thing she has ever done in her life. "I have something very interesting to say about this. I think that the best thing I have done was when my son went to prison the first time. In the midst of the immense pain I felt . . . and only if one has gone through it, can one know what it is like. First of all, you are totally lost; I did not know anything about bail, I did not know that there were so many prisons in New York state. They sent him to Attica, and I used to take the bus to go see him—nine hours. . . . How ashamed I felt because, as we say, they do their sentence inside; we do it outside. When we would travel together, we became friends because everyone is in the same situation. There were mothers who did not know English. The first ones to take advantage of you are the lawyers. . . . I went to a workshop about prisons, and I learned that the archdiocese has an apostolate with prisoners. I was able to use all of this to help others. I ran into a nun who told me, "Do not forget that your son is going to come back to society. If you forget him, he will not be able to come back. You can be useful. You can help mothers who find themselves in this situation, and they do not know what to do."

"I would take my son huge packages that he could share with others. . . . I was able to turn my pain to help others who were in the same situation and did not know where to go, had no financial means; there were times when through my son I would send them money. That was partially because the Lord gave me strength at that time, and I was able to go beyond myself; I was able to see that there were worse needs than mine. I was able to do something in the name of God for others. And, even up to now, as I continue to be in the same situation—to be able to help others who need it. We as Christians have the moral obligation of lending them a hand, no matter how repugnant and undesirable they are to us. Behind each one of them there is a mother who suffers. I do not allow anyone to say anything bad about my son."

Given the death of two of her sons, the imprisonment of a third son, and the death of her husband, it is very important to notice what María considers has been the worst experience in her life. "For me a terrible moment in my life—it is the only negative thing that has happened to me, besides the personal things—was to be accused unjustly of something and not even to have the opportunity to defend myself. I have lived in the same building for twenty-seven or twenty-eight years. I have this custom that when I clean, I put on music and really get carried away cleaning. I love perfume, so I buy all the cleaning fluids that come out on the market that smell nice and put it in the water. I also always clean the hallway outside my apartment—and everything smells really nice. A West Indian woman lived on my floor, and I noticed that she would go by and not say anything. One day it really bothered me, so I said to her, 'Hazel, did I do something that offended you, because you go by me, and you do not even say hello.' She answered me, 'Oh yes, I am happy you asked. When are you going to stop doing witchcraft outside my door?' With the experience that I had growing up—how much I hate spiritism—I said to her, 'How can you say that? What I do is clean the hallway with nice smelling liquid, and it benefits all the neighbors.' She did not give me a chance to apologize or anything. She just walked away. I think she is the only enemy I have ever had. I stopped cleaning, but she never looked at me again. When my children died . . . she never came to my apartment. . . . Her accusation has always hurt me because she never allowed me to apologize, she never inquired to see if what she thought was true. . . . It hurt me so deeply to be accused unjustly. She had been prosecutor and judge and did not give me a chance to explain. I have known so many people, and everyone likes me. And what this woman did to me—if she would have slapped me, it would have hurt less."

Olivia

It took Olivia a while to be able to focus on the best and worst experiences in her life. After a while, she told the group the following. "For me the best thing has been to come to know who I am. Then I can help others, I can serve. To come to know my value as a person—that I am important and worth something, and I am not just a part of someone else—that is the best for me.

"The worst is lack of justice. No one should just be silent because then the problem gets bigger, and how can you help that person if the person is not willing to fight? If you do not fight back, that is the worst possible thing. When one suffers injustice, one has to defend one's rights.

"The other very bad thing has been the way I have ignored my body. I regret that I have not taken adequate care of myself. About six months ago when I was helping at a friend's house, my hands went numb. I went to the doctor, and they wanted to do all sorts of tests. I said, 'No; first give me some time, and let's see how things go.' It was God teaching me to take care of my body. The numbness is completely gone, and I am fine."

Margarita

It took a while for Margarita to be able to think of something she would consider "the best." Her sense is that so many good things have happened in her life that it is not easy to focus on one. However, prodded on by the enabler, eventually she came up with one. "The best thing that has happened to me is that a car hit me and I am still alive. I have told people that during the days following the accident I could not comprehend that I was alive. I knew I was alive, but I could not understand that I was alive and nothing had happened to me. For two months or so I had this strange sense that I was not altogether here. It was such a surprise to find that I was alive.

"The best thing I have done is that I have been able to bring children into the world. Since I could not do what I wanted to do, to be a nun, when my daughter was born, I named her after Our Lady of Charity, and I wanted my daughter to be a nun but that has not happened. But that I was able to multiply, without offending anyone, that was very good.

"The worst thing that has happened to me . . . I am so grateful for what I have that I cannot think of much that has been bad. The only thing is when I was not able to go see my mother when she was dying. I tried, and they did not let me go; to lose her without being able to see her one last time, that was very bad. I feel happy about what I have done and what has happened to me. I help anyone who asks me; I feel satisfied."

Recurring Themes

The understanding of morality prevalent in the lives of these women is oriented toward family and community. For all of them "the good" has to do with their obligations to others; for Inez it is her commitment to the community; for Adela and Marta it has to do with their obligation towards their children. For Lupe "the good" has to do with being the best she can be, but she sees that as basically depending on, and being used for, the people of the community. The same is true of Olivia. To come to know her value as a person is the best thing for her because she can then help others, serve them. María considers the peak of her goodness to be her having turned the pain of her son being in prison into an opportunity to help others. Also, she admires in herself her loyalty to her son. For Margarita goodness is tied up with life—both the life she has in spite of being hit by a car and the life she gave her children at birth. Their understandings certainly give clear indication of what motivates them, of what they understand salvation to be, what their heaven will be like.

When speaking about evil, what concerns them are social issues. Evil for Inez is whatever takes away from her the source of her vision out of which grows her commitment: her self-worth based on the goodness of her culture. For Margarita evil has to do with not having control over her own life—not being able to go back to Cuba to see her dying mother. Lupe connects evil with not recognizing her goodness and her commitment. Several times she mentioned how much she is hurt by comments implying that people do not trust that what she is doing is for the good of the community. María's sense of what is evil closely parallels Lupe's. To be accused unjustly and not to be allowed to explain what she had done—not to be able to defend herself—that for her is evil. And for Olivia evil has to do with lack of justice and lack of courage to defend oneself. She has come to understand that there is a connection between what is not good and disregard for her own body.

Adela echoes what Inez and Lupe have said linking evil to destruction of self-worth when she mentions—and this was not the only time she talked about it—how hurt she is by the contempt of the Anglos. For her and Marta evil is not doing what is good for their children, which is what makes them happy. Marta's sense of loyalty parallels Adela's understanding of doing for others. Later in the conversation, Marta identifies self-centeredness as the one thing she would like to change in the world. Sin is not a matter of disobedience but of not being for others. Not going to church is not a sin. But not to care for the children or the community—that is a sin, a crime! And the women take direct responsibility for what they do or do not do. Though they have a certain sense of predestination, they do not blame anyone but themselves for what goes wrong. On the other hand, God is given credit for the good that they do, the good that occurs in their lives.

Theology cannot ignore the ethical sense of these Hispanic Women. Their understandings have direct consequences not only for moral theology, but also for soteriology, which deals with the doctrine of salvation—the understanding of sin and grace being central to it. Hispanic Women's religious understandings also have to be taken seriously by pastoral theology, which should be understood as the study of the participation of the church in the struggle for liberation of Hispanic Women.

Entendimientos sobre la moral de la Mujer Hispana

Este capítulo de nuevo cita a las siete Mujeres Hispanas que hablaron en un capítulo previo. Lo que aquí dicen tiene grandes consecuencias, no sólo para la teología moral, sino también para la teología pastoral y lo que se entiende por salvación.

La moralidad en las vidas de estas Mujeres Hispanas tiene que ver por arriba de todo con la familia y la comunidad. Para todas ellas «lo bueno» tiene que ver con las obligaciones que tienen para con los demás. Para Inez «lo bueno» tiene que ver con su compromiso con la comunidad. Para Adela y Marta tiene que ver con como ellas actúan con sus hijas e hijos. Para Lupe «lo bueno» es lo que le permite y capacita para «ser más», pero eso depende de la comunidad y de su comportamiento hacia ellos. Olivia piensa igual. Lo mejor que le ha pasado en la vida es descubrir el valor que ella tiene como persona, porque así puede ayudar a otros, servirlos. María considera que «lo más monumental» que ha hecho en su vida es haber podido usar el dolor de tener un hijo encarcelado para ayudar a otros. También admira en sí misma lo fiel que le ha sido a ese hijo. Para Margarita «lo bueno» y «la vida» están profundamente vinculados—la vida que tiene a pesar de haber sido atropellada por un carro y la vida que ella les dió a su hija e hijo al momento de nacer.

Cuando hablan de la maldad, lo que les interesa son males sociales. Para Inez la maldad es cualquier cosa que la separa de la visión que le inspira su compromiso con el pueblo; su valor en sus propios ojos está basado en el valor que le da a su cultura. Para Margarita la maldad tiene que ver con no tener control sobre su propia vida—no haber podido regresar a Cuba para ver a su mamá gravemente enferma. Lupe ve una conexión entre la maldad y no reconocer lo bueno y hermoso de su compromiso con el pueblo. Varias veces mencionó lo mucho que le duelen los comentarios de algunas personas que le dan a entender que no creen que lo que ella hace es por el bien de la comunidad. El concepto de María de la maldad es muy semejante al de Lupe. Que la hayan acusado injustamente sin dejarla explicar sus acciones, que no la hayan dejado defenderse—eso es lo que es «lo más malo». Y para Olivia la maldad tiene que ver con la falta de justicia y el no tener la valentía necesaria para defenderse. Ultimamente ella ha empezado a comprender la conexión que existe entre «lo que no es bueno» y el no cuidarse físicamente.

Para Adela la maldad es algo parecido a lo que es para Inez y Lupe—ella relaciona la maldad con la destrucción de su valor propio causada por el desprecio de los anglos. Para ella, al igual que para Marta, la maldad tiene que ver con no ser buenas con sus hijas e hijos. Más tarde en la conversación Marta identificó el egoísmo y el estar concentrado en una misma como algo que ella quisiera cambiar.

El pecado no es desobedecer, sino el no ser para otros. El no ir a la iglesia no es un pecado. Pero el no cuidar de sus hijas e hijos y de la comunidad—eso es pecado. Y estas Mujeres Hispanas se responsabilizan por lo que hacen o dejan de hacer. Aunque tienen un cierto sentido de fatalismo no acusan a nadie que no sea ellas mismas por lo malo que les pasa. Sin embargo, le dan a Dios crédito por lo bueno que ellas hacen y lo que ocurre en sus vidas.

Chapter 5

METHODOLOGY AND TASK
OF HISPANIC WOMEN'S
LIBERATION THEOLOGY

The methodology of Hispanic Women's Liberation Theology has to be necessarily different from those of other liberation theologies given the specific nature of Hispanic Women's experience. At the same time, because Hispanic Women's Liberation Theology is a praxis, its task is an important theological consideration both enlightening and being the basis of the theological discourse.

The Method

Hispanic Women's Liberation Theology, like all praxis, consists of two interlinked moments: action and reflection. It is difficult to speak about these two moments without falling into a false dichotomy and/or dualism. Any separation of action and reflection when speaking about praxis is only a heuristic device needed because of the limitations of human language. Hispanic Women are increasingly aware of how false and evil is any attempt to separate action from reflection. Their physical participation in programs and/or actions is often sought, but they are seldom asked to be involved in deciding and/or designing their content. This is a way of victimizing Hispanic Women, for they are not allowed and/or invited to participate in the reflective moment of praxis. Because of this, their actions on behalf of the community often have not been part of their own process of conscientization/liberation.

Hispanic Women's Liberation Theology is totally committed to the action side of praxis; Hispanic Women's Liberation Theology is likewise totally committed to and adamantly insistent on the reflective moment of praxis. It is because of the present situation of Hispanic Women—the way they are treated by society at large and by many of the leaders in the Hispanic community—that Hispanic Women's Liberation Theology has the very specific task of insisting on the reflective moment of praxis. The method and style of reflection not only greatly influence the praxis—the doing theology—but are also intrinsic parts of it.

The method used by Hispanic Women's Liberation Theology is dialogic. Dialogue is a horizontal relationship that involves communication and intercommunication. It refers to a "relation of 'empathy' between two 'poles' who are engaged in a joint search." The method, therefore, has to bring together the content of the search and both poles involved in the dialogue. The content of the search is the liberation of Hispanic Women. In Hispanic Women's Liberation Theology the two poles are the community and the enabler(s) of the reflection. It is most important that the coming together of the content and the poles be facilitated by an enabler who is a member of the community—someone "participating intensely in the forward march of the people. . . ." When the enabler is not herself a part of the community—having some vested interest in the liberation of those involved because her liberation is connected to the liberation of the others in the group—the dialogue becomes dishonest, the group is objectified, and theology becomes a tool of oppression.[1]

Because Hispanic Women's Liberation Theology as a praxis strives for the liberation of Hispanic Women, necessarily it has to be involved in an ongoing process of conscientization. In Hispanic Women's Liberation Theology, conscientization is understood to mean an ongoing process of critical reflection on action, which leads to a critical awareness. This critical awareness is intrinsic to being agents of one's own history—self-determining human beings. Because the critical reflection is one of the elements/moments of praxis, the critical awareness that results cannot be separated from action.

One cannot change consciousness outside of praxis. But it must be emphasized that the praxis by which consciousness is changed is not only action but
action and reflection. Thus there is a unity between practice and theory in
which both are constructed, shaped and reshaped in constant movement from
practice to theory, then back to a new practice. . . . [Conscientization]
must . . . be a critical attempt to reveal reality. . . . It must . . . be related to
political involvement. There is no conscientization if the result is not the
conscious action of the oppressed as an exploited social class, struggling for
liberation. What is more, no one conscientizes anyone else. The educator and
the people together conscientize themselves, thanks to the dialectical movement which relates critical reflection on past action to the continuous
struggle.[2]

The process for the reflection moment of the praxis has to take into
consideration and be geared to enabling actively this process of conscientization. However, it is important to realize that the action
moment of praxis is just as critical—as important and enabling of
conscientization—as the reflection moment. The process of reflection
starts with action and leads to action, but it is also inherently action,
for it is instrumental in enabling the conscientization without which
liberation is not possible.

The figure below shows the process used for doing Hispanic
Women's Liberation Theology.[3] The process involves several "movements," having as their goal the development of critical consciousness. A spiral is used instead of a circle to indicate that it is an
ongoing, open process, during which other movements might and
could happen or be added.

The left side of the figure shows how these four movements are
interwoven and interfacing. They cannot always be isolated; most of
the time one is not understood if all are not understood.

Process Used in Doing Hispanic Women's Liberation Theology

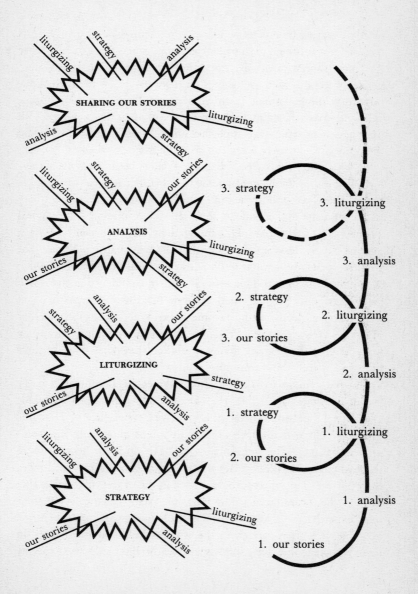

Telling Our Stories

Given Hispanic Women's strong sense of relationships and community, storytelling is very natural to them. Consequently, it is nothing new for them to share stories; what is new is a growing sense that these shared stories are important—politically important—and not mere gossip, as they have often pejoratively been called. Four important things happen in this movement. By telling their stories, Hispanic Women claim that the events of their lives, along with themselves as persons, are important and relevant. Second, by placing their stories "out there for all to see," their stories become "object" upon which they can reflect. Hispanic Women become agents of their own history. As these women come to know their own stories, an "I-know-what-I-am-talking-about" attitude takes over, filling them with confidence and enhancing their self-determination—their moral agency. Third, the parallels among their stories become obvious, making Hispanic Women realize that the personal is political, that what happens to them has to do with structural factors about which they have little to say. This also gives them confidence in their own experience, thus helping them to know that their interpretation of what happens to them and around them is not wrong—that other Hispanic Women share it. Finally, as they share their stories, they are affirming the ongoing divine revelation that takes place in their lives and within the community.

One of the main goals of Hispanic Women's Liberation Theology is self-determination. The real or concrete context of Hispanic Women's Liberation Theology is the lived experience of Hispanic Women. Telling their stories brings this lived experience into common awareness. The questions to be dealt with in the process of theologizing surface here. But the telling of the stories yields more than the questions; the vocabulary used in the process of theologizing must be the vocabulary used by Hispanic Women as they relate their lived experiences. Academic theological language and official church language are often foreign to the women and/or might trigger in them responses they have internalized as the right response expected from them, instead of what they really think and believe. Religious language, on the other hand, is used repeatedly by Hispanic Women in the telling of their stories because it is commonly used in their everyday lives. This religious language should form the bulk of the language used by Hispanic Women's Liberation Theology.

Analysis

Analysis is perhaps the most difficult of the "movements" because of the complexity of the oppression of Hispanic Women. Analysis is an arduous task, but skipping it or failing to do it seriously and in-depth will prevent Hispanic Women from attaining critical consciousness, which in turn will give rise to magical solutions such as "we need to pray more." Often, when analysis is treated lightly, so-called enablers will conclude that the people are not ready or are not capable of understanding or doing something when, in reality, the group is always willing and capable if the analysis is based on the lived experience of the members of the group. However, if the enabler imposes frameworks of analysis foreign to the people's experience, the group will balk. They will fall back into a posture of silence, which is not a sign of their lack of ability to think or to express themselves, but of their unwillingness to be manipulated into understanding their own experience in a way not born of that same experience. For example, in November of 1983 about twelve hundred women met in Chicago for a conference: "Womenchurch speaks." Ten percent were Hispanics. As part of the program, a presentation was made by a woman member of the Sandinista government who denounced the United States and asked the assembled to support the Sandinista government. The response among the Hispanic Women was not too positive. Among the reasons for this are the following:

a) Hispanic Women have very little or no information except what the conventional means of communication gives them. We found the Hispanic Women tremendously responsible in not being willing to endorse "the first different thing that they hear."

b) There was no process at the conference for an analysis of what the Nicaraguan woman was saying; there was no way for Hispanic Women to come to see the relation between their oppression and the way the United States behaves toward Nicaragua.

In this situation, an analysis born out of the lived experience of the people was lacking.

The theme/content questions used in the analysis should change according to the situation at hand. The questions are always posed to enable the people to understand the "moods and motivations" operating in their lives. That is why, no matter what the situation, two key questions for the analysis are "why" and "what else"—"why do you think this happened this way instead of that? What else—is there another reason for what happened?" The former question is obvious, but the latter is often not used. However, an analysis that does not go beyond the obvious in order to make the connections between the personal and the political, the Hispanic community and the structures of society—to make the connections among different kinds of oppressions—such an analysis will yield strategies resulting in band-aid solutions instead of in structural change.

Liturgizing

Liturgizing, of all the "movements," is the one that can be less confined into a specific moment. Since liturgy has to do with the aesthetic side of our humanity, it is always present, though hardly ever acknowledged. When the term *aesthetics* is understood as "perception that is characterized by feeling *reasoned* and *feeling* reason,"[4] then one can call the Hispanic culture, and Hispanic people in general, highly aesthetic. The Hispanic culture places a high value on feelings and emotions and the consequent ease of showing and sharing them. This is one of the main reasons why, for Hispanic Women, liturgizing is a natural and spontaneous way of relating to the divine.

Liturgizing as one of the "movements" of the doing of theology is important for Hispanic Women for several reasons. First, by making liturgy a part of the process of doing theology, the sense of unworthiness Hispanic Women feel when they participate in official worship services is negated. This sense of unworthiness is generated by the many different and tangible ways in which liturgical ministers of official worship services are projected as "holier" or "more worthy" than the Hispanic Women sitting in the pews. Second, in the process of doing theology, Hispanic Women affirm that they are agents of their own history and can, therefore, decide how best to represent the divine, be in touch with the divine—and that is what liturgy is about.

Liturgizing is also a hope-full experience. It goes beyond language, which is very much controlled by the oppressive foreign culture in which Hispanic Women live. It provides the opportunity to announce the envisioned future while denouncing the oppressive present. Finally, liturgizing frees and encourages the religious imagination of Hispanic Women—an important power for liberation and transformation at both the personal and societal levels.[5]

Strategizing

Strategizing is never to be understood as something added to theology and not an intrinsic part of it. The strategizing "movement," like the other three, is intrinsic to the doing of theology. Hispanic Women have a sense that they should do something, and the reason for this doing, as already indicated, is often a religious one. It is necessary to keep in mind three considerations regarding strategizing. The goal of all strategies is not to find ways of participating in present structures that are patriarchal and, therefore, oppressive; instead, the goal is to change those oppressive structures. Strategies, therefore, focus on equalizing power so as to bring about the kairos, the moment full of the presence of the divine—the moment when "power-over" can be transformed into "power-to." Power-over is the kind of power that is most operative in the world today; it controls, dominates, coerces, whether openly or through subterfuges such as advertisement. Power-to is the power exercised by persons and institutions involved in the struggles for liberation; it has to do with capacity for self-determination, enablement, creativity—all in the context of a community and its common good.

A second consideration to be kept in mind is the need to design overall strategies that must be evaluated constantly—they have to be seen as part of an ongoing process. This means that the particularity of a given situation might well call for tactics that do not ignore, but might temporarily supersede, any and all general strategies. At the same time, strategies of a given struggle always include consideration of their effect on other situations of oppression. Without this consideration, horizontal violence among different oppressed groups easily develops; then the oppressors are the only ones to benefit from the situation.

Finally, strategies have to come from the community, since only the community involved knows the risks that it is willing to take. Different members of the community have different contributions to make to the struggle and are at different points in the process of conscientization. Therefore, strategies must include a variety of modes of implementation and the capability for use in different circumstances. When they are implementable in different circumstances, strategies can be carried out first within the person herself, as a challenge to mind-sets and oppressive patterns of behavior, which the socialization process imposes on Hispanic Women and which they internalize. These strategies also can be put into effect within the primary community of the person—helping in the restructuring of relationships. Third, strategies have to be implementable in the wider group to which Hispanic Women relate, such as work or organizations to which they belong.

That strategies have/should have a variety of modes of implementation will assure their success and the participation of a broad spectrum of the community in carrying them out. Strategies could have, for example, an educational prong that promotes conscientization. They can also have an advocacy aspect that establishes dialogue with oppressive structures and persons. The same strategy should have a third prong: witness actions such as civil disobedience and ecclesial disobedience, which both strengthen the community and make known the struggle of Hispanic Women.

The Task

The task of Hispanic Women's Liberation Theology is to further the liberation of Hispanic Women. Liberation is an ongoing process that involves three levels of meaning of one complex process.

In the first place, liberation expresses the aspirations of oppressed peoples and social classes, emphasizing the conflictual aspect of the economic, social, and political process which puts them at odds with wealthy nations and oppressive classes. . . .

At a deeper level, liberation can be applied to an understanding of history. Man [sic] is seen as assuming conscious responsibility of his [sic] own destiny. . . . In this perspective the unfolding of man's [sic] dimensions is demanded—a man [sic] who makes himself [sic] throughout his [sic] life and throughout history.[6]

Third, liberation enables Hispanic Women to deal with their religious understandings and practices in such a way that they recognize them as the source of their presence and action in history. Liberation enables Hispanic Women to articulate what they have often lived "unconsciously": it is their sense of the divine in their lives that gives them strength for the struggle—a struggle that is not a part of life but life itself.[7]

Undoubtedly, because of the different levels of meaning in the process of liberation, Hispanic Women's Liberation Theology is a subversive praxis. It does not accommodate itself to church or academic structures but rather seeks to change them so that Hispanic Women will be able to participate fully in them. As a praxis, Hispanic Women's Liberation Theology has to insist on the reflective moment, which is so important in the ongoing process of critical awareness. Without this critical awareness, there is no conscientization and, therefore, no possibility of liberation. Reflection is also intrinsic to self-definition. Only by a firm grasp of who they are—their religious and cultural roots—and who they want to be—their hopes and dreams of liberation—can Hispanic Women begin to be self-determining. Furthermore, the possibility of being self-determining depends partially on being able to influence the norm. That will never happen without reflection, without a critical awareness that will enable them to lay aside "all forms of false consciousness . . . and learn to discern what is of perennial value in their own cultural traditions."[8]

The Theologians

Hispanic Women's Liberation Theology as a praxis is done by the community and not just by one or two persons. Hispanic Women protesting the lack of city services in the South Bronx, emptying a bag of trash on the desk of the city official who could order the garbage picked up more frequently in the area where the women live—that is doing Hispanic Women's Liberation Theology. A woman struggling in a meeting controlled by Hispanic men to pass a resolution that would insure a certain percentage of women in each of the delegations to an important national meeting—that is doing Hispanic Women's Liberation Theology. Four women testifying in front of a group of Roman Catholic bishops about the oppression of Hispanic Women in church as well as in society, finishing their presentation by giving each of the bishops a stone and telling them, "We have asked for bread and you have given us stone. Put these stones on your altars when you celebrate Eucharist and remember us Hispanic Women, struggling for our liberation and the liberation of our people"—that is doing Hispanic Women's Liberation Theology.

But the reflection that led to such actions, reflection about self-identity, about our participation in making decisions that affect us and our families, about our willingness to risk—doing such reflection is also doing Hispanic Women's Liberation Theology. Meeting after an action to analyze what has been done, to evaluate how each one involved performed assigned tasks, to hold accountable those who have participated in a community action/project—participating in such meetings is doing Hispanic Women's Liberation Theology. To gather, to reflect on how the nature of Hispanic Women's involvement either reflects or goes against important values and religious understandings—such reflection is doing Hispanic Women's Liberation Theology.

Hispanic Women's Liberation Theology as a praxis is done by the community, each one contributing to the process of doing theology according to her own gifts: combining her natural ability, opportunity, and her generosity for the good of the community. All gifts are of equal value. No gift is better than another one; no gift is more valuable, more holy, more worthy of respect than another. At a given moment, because of a particular need, one gift might be more useful than another, but that does not make it more important. To place the gifts of the people of the community in any hierarchical gradation is to do violence to the community. One of the intrinsic elements of the community is an equalization of power. To see anyone's gift as more important is to do away with equality, is to permit the use of individual gifts for claiming power over the rest of the community. Anyone using her gift in such fashion has destroyed the gift because it is not being used any longer for the common good; gifts are gifts only insofar as they are used for the good of the community.

In any community there is a great variety of gifts. Some of the members of the community have the gift of gathering the folk; others are the physical and/or spiritual nurturers of the group; others are powerful speakers; and others are prophets listening to the hidden hopes of the people and proclaiming them. Some can move the community to prayer and worship; others are leaders of action; others quietly pursue the common good by being always ready to participate; others are writers; and others are teachers/learners—enablers. Among the latter are those who enable the group in the reflective moment of praxis, who lead the community in reflecting on the "moods and motivations" that move the community, who enable the community to understand that its daily struggle for survival is not separate from its religious understandings, sentiments, beliefs. The Hispanic Women with this gift of enablement, as well as those with the gift of gathering what the community is saying, writing it down, and making it known are indeed "theological technicians."

"Theological technicians" are those who are "in possession of certain technical competences in exegesis, social sciences, languages, archaeology, or history and who offer(s) these findings in these different fields to the real theologians to help them in the act of interpreting reality from . . . (their) perspective. . . ."[9]

Theological technicians, as well as other members of the community with specific knowledge, must not hoard what they know—often a ploy used to achieve privileged status within the community. On the contrary, theological technicians should make it their goal to help others learn these same skills so as to enrich the community and its praxis.

What is the task of the theological technician who is the enabler? First, enablers of the reflective moments have to understand their task very clearly so as not to objectify the group and set themselves up as the authority. The task of the enabler is to lead the participants in the group "to grasp the knowledge we all have."[10] The enabler has to both see herself and be seen as a member of the group. She might suggest the questions—some of the questions, the starting questions—but she also has to be willing to share with the group, to become vulnerable in order to learn with the group, from the group. The enabler has the responsibility of insisting on critical reflection. It is not a matter of just telling stories, of just relating what happened; it is a matter of coming to understand the reasons behind the events in the lives of Hispanic Women. Only then will a critical consciousness be developed by the group as a whole and by each of the members of the group in particular. The enabler has to push the group continually to make the connections between what different members of the group are saying, between what they are saying and their religious understandings and actions, between the understandings of this group and those of other groups. Finally, the enabler has to be sure that the reflection of the community is gathered and recorded, as it is of great importance for that community to continue to deal with what they have surfaced during the time spent together; in the same way, the reflection of the community is important for other communities also struggling for liberation. The reflections of the community need to be given a voice in order to claim a place as part of the norm of society.

The recorder/writer, whether or not she is the enabler, also has to be a member of the group. Unless she is an intrinsic member of the community and understands that her own liberation is linked to the liberation of the community about which she is writing, she runs the risk of objectifying the group, of using what the community has said to make her own individual points. The recorder/writer, therefore, has a most important task; she is accountable to the community for saying what the community has said and not making the community say, through her writings, what it did not say. At the same time, she is also accountable to the community for making what the community has said understandable to the other communities of struggle and even to the dominant group in order to challenge it. Thus, because her writing is addressed to several audiences, the task of the recorder/writer is enormously complicated. How can the material speak to Hispanic Women and the Hispanic community at large and, at the same time, say something to and/or be understood by theological communities of other cultures and oppressed groups? Regardless of which community she is addressing, the recorder/writer must keep in mind at all times that her main community of accountability is the community of Hispanic Women.

How does the recorder/writer deal with the issue of making both audible and understandable the voice of the community instead of thinking that she is "being" or is "giving" a voice to the community? In order not to lose the truth and vitality generated by the process, the writer needs to understand the process not as a consultation, but as *doing* theology. The material gathered should not be violated by imposing the writer's analysis and theological constructs on it and/or using the material gathered from the reflection of the community as examples backing up what the writer wants to say.

In order not to fall into this objectification of the reflection of the community, the writing process needs to follow certain criteria:

- The writer needs to write in a very simple way, using extensive direct quotes from what the community has said.[11] The analysis should be geared to explaining what the women have said.
- The material needs to be organized rather than systematized according to some preconceived construct. It is not a matter of imposing a systematic grid on it but of organizing it so that its meaning is readily accessible and reflects accurately the community's reflection.
- The organization should be around central words/ideas that are repeated often in the conversation and carry emotional weight. Two important keys to this emotional weight are: When do the women cry? When do they speak in English and when in Spanish? Both the expressions of emotion and the choice of language give most important clues as to what is intrinsic to the women's lives and what are foreign, nonorganic understandings.
- The relationship among these frequently repeated central ideas/words has to be carefully considered. Do they relate dialectically, sympathetically, controversially?
- The imagery used by the women has to be central in the writing. The imagery should stand on its own; its interpretation should neither overwhelm it, simplify it, nor adapt it.[12]

Once the recorder/writer has finished her task, the material should be reviewed by a representative number of the women who have participated in the praxis. This is done in order to ensure faithfulness of the written word to the understandings and experiences of the group. If the group members cannot relate directly to what has been written, the writing needs revision. Second, they must see what has been written as their own. The litmus test for this will be the future use of the written material by the community. Third, the community doing theology needs also to decide how it wants to use what has been written—is it best to use it only internally or would it be a good strategy to go public with their reflections? If the material is going to be made public, it needs to be studied by members of other communities who stand in solidarity with Hispanic Women to ensure that what has been written is a voice that can be understood but cannot be used against these other communities of struggle.

To claim that the community of Hispanic Women is the real theologian and to insist that those academically trained are but theological technicians—organic theologians themselves insofar as they are members of the theologizing community—these are intrinsic elements of Hispanic Women's Liberation Theology. The community of Hispanic Women is the true theologian; in no way does Hispanic Women's Liberation Theology attempt to minimize or see the task of the community as less important or less central to the process of doing theology than the task of the theological technicians.[13] This does not mean that there might not be a proper place and function for academic theology—a theology done by technicians for a community of which they are not a part or a "general" theology based on the belief that the technician's understandings are "objective" and, therefore, universally valid. Frankly, to affirm or deny the existence or importance of such a theology is irrelevant to Hispanic Women. This is made evident by the fact that many Hispanic Women have lived their religion mostly outside the official churches with which academic theology deals and that they have ignored the language of such a theology. Such irrelevance is a warning to academic theologians about claiming to be "voice of the voiceless."[14]

Evaluating the Task

The task of the writer as described in the previous section includes what constitutes an evaluation for Hispanic Women's Liberation Theology: submitting the text to the community of Hispanic Women in order for them to see if it is faithful to their experience, if they can understand what is being said. Does the language adequately disclose "an authentic dimension of [their] experiences as selves"? Is what is being said true? Does it explain "how a particular concept (e.g., time, space, self, or God) functions as a fundamental 'belief' or 'condition of possibility' of all [their] experience"?[15] Does it clearly and unequivocally explain the religious dimension of the moods and motivations that move them to action and give them reason for hope? Is what has been written an appropriate understanding of their sense and experience of Christianity?[16]

Though this analysis by Hispanic Women is the core and deciding factor in the evaluation of Hispanic Women's Liberation Theology, it also requires an evaluation by people outside the community in order to ascertain if what has been written can be understood clearly by the other receiving communities. Persons from other oppressed groups standing in solidarity with Hispanic Women—those willing to understand not only with the head but also with the heart, willing to enter into the experience of Hispanic Women as much as they can—are the ones, besides Hispanic Women, to critique, to evaluate what has been written. The task is not to judge whether it is right or wrong but, again, to ascertain that what is being said will be grasped adequately by others. It is important for questions pertaining to strategy to figure in their critique. Given the way of presenting the material, is it going to gain some attention, a foot in the door? Is it going to impact society at large at least in a small way?

This is extremely important because, since the task of Hispanic Women's Liberation Theology is the liberation of women, doing theology has to operate at the three levels of meaning included in the sense of liberation. Is Hispanic Women's Liberation Theology contributing to the political, economic, and social liberation of Hispanic Women? Is it enabling Hispanic Women to assume conscious responsibility for their own history? Does it elucidate, explain how their religious understandings and their "Christianity" motivate them to action?[17]

Hispanic Women's Liberation Theology has been born. As a process and a praxis, it is always being birthed by Hispanic Women who struggle for liberation and for whom *la vida es la lucha* [life is the struggle]. But Hispanic Women's Liberation Theology also does the birthing—it births hope and a vision of the future in which all peoples will be free because Hispanic Women are free.

Metodología y tarea de «teología de la liberación de la Mujer Hispana»

Debido a que la experiencia de la Mujer Hispana tiene características propias, la metodología de la teología de la liberación de la Mujer Hispana tiene que ser necesariamente diferente a la de las otras teologías de la liberación. A la misma vez, debido a que la teología de la liberación de la Mujer Hispana es una praxis, su tarea es una consideración teológica muy importante que esclarece a la vez que forma parte de la base del discurso teológico.

Método

Al igual que toda praxis, la teología de la liberación de la Mujer Hispana que aquí se presenta, tiene dos momentos que están entrelazados y que son parte intrínseca el uno del otro, la acción y la reflexión. Estos dos momentos no existen separados el uno del otro; no existe dicotomía alguna entre ellos. Hablar de ellos por separado es un método heurístico impuesto por las limitaciones del lenguaje humano.

El método usado por esta teología es el diálogo—una relación horizontal que incluye la comunicación y la intercomunicación. El diálogo tiene que ver con establecer una empatía entre dos polos que juntos participan en una búsqueda. Lo que busca este diálogo es la liberación de las Mujeres Hispanas. En este teología los dos polos son la comunidad y los miembros de esa misma comunidad que facilitan la reflexión. Esta reflexión es parte del proceso de concientización—un proceso de reflexión crítica sobre la acción que nunca termina y que lleva a una comprensión crítica de la realidad. Esta comprensión crítica es lo que permite que uno sea sujeto de su propia historia—que uno se auto-determine. Porque esta reflexión crítica es uno de los momentos y elementos de la praxis, la reflexión no existe separada de la acción. El proceso de reflexión empieza con la acción y lleva a la acción, pero también es en sí mismo acción ya que es instrumento de concientización y sin ésta última no es posible la liberación.

El método usado por esta teología de la liberación de la Mujer Hispana tiene cuatro movimientos que constantemente se entrelazan y combinan: relato de sus experiencias, análisis, liturgia, y estrategia. El relato de sus experiencias hace posible que las Mujeres Hispanas se den cuenta de que lo que a ellas les pasa es importante. Al oírse a sí mismas las Mujeres Hispanas pueden reflexionar sobre sus propias vidas, y esto les permite tener una cierta seguridad sobre quiénes son y lo que piensan. El compartir sus historias rompe el aislamiento que muchas veces sienten y así llegan a ver que lo que les pasa es resultado, no de su incompetencia o culpa personal, sino de estructuras opresivas.

El momento del análisis es probablemente el más difícil, debido a los múltiples elementos que se conjugan para oprimir a la Mujer Hispana. Pero hay que insistir en él ya que sin análisis se cae en soluciones fáciles o en una postura silenciosa que indica impotencia. El análisis tiene que partir de la experiencia de las Mujeres Hispanas, y no realizarse de acuerdo a esquemas sociológicos o económicos abstractos.

La liturgia es el movimiento que menos se puede limitar en un momento definido. La liturgia tiene que ver con la estética y por lo tanto siempre está presente, aunque es raramente reconocida. La liturgia es un raciocinio que se *siente* y un sentimiento que se *razona*. Debido a que los sentimientos tienen un valor cultural muy elevado entre las Mujeres Hispanas, ellas tienen gran capacidad para expresarse litúrgicamente. Los momentos litúrgicos diseñados por las Mujeres Hispanas les demuestran que sí se pueden acercar a lo divino sin intermediarios, que sí son dignas de dirigirse personalmente a Dios.

Las estrategias nunca deben de ser vista como algo que se añade al final del proceso teológico. Las estrategias tienen que ver con ese impulso revolucionario que es parte intrínseca del sentido religioso de la Mujer Hispana. Las estrategias tratan de deshacer estructuras opresivas; tienen que nacer pues de la comunidad, pues sólo los miembros de la comunidad saben cuánto están dispuestas a arriesgarse.

La teología de la liberación de la Mujer Hispana cree firmemente que los verdaderos teólogos son las Mujeres Hispanas que participan en la lucha por la liberación. Cuando las Mujeres Hispanas del Sur del Bronx protestan la poca frecuencia con que se recoge la basura están haciendo teología. Las Mujeres Hispanas que se dirigen a un grupo de obispos para hablar sobre las necesidades de su comunidad están haciendo teología. Pero también es hacer teología el reflexionar que precedió y tuvo lugar después de estas acciones.

Como praxis, esta teología de la liberación de la Mujer Hispana es una labor comunitaria, y cada miembro de la comunidad contribuye de acuerdo a sus dones y de acuerdo a las necesidades de la comunidad. Al hacer teología se necesitan miembros de la comunidad que facilitan tanto el momento reflexivo como la acción en sí misma. También se necesita a alguien que escriba lo que la comunidad dice y hace. Tantos los que facilitan como los que escriben son «técnicos teológicos» que hacen posible que otras comunidades escuchen y sepan lo que las Mujeres Hispanas están haciendo y diciendo. Esto hace posible que los entendimientos, costumbres, y prácticas religiosos de las Mujeres Hispanas se conviertan un día en parte integral de la norma de la sociedad en general.

APPENDIX

The following questions were used to enable the discussions with Hispanic Women about their religious understandings. Neither the ordering of the questions nor the language used was always the same.

The questions were not invented by the enablers but rather are the result of many years of listening to what is important in the lives of Hispanic Women. Each and every time they are used, the questions are modified. Some of the subquestions serve as an organizing framework for the materials gathered.

The religious understandings of Hispanic Women are relevant to their day-to-day lives. Therefore, reflection on any action in which they are engaged yields rich theological material. These questions are but one way, perhaps the least important way, in which Hispanic Women's religious understandings can be fleshed out. The theological value of the responses to these questions depends, among other things, on whether or not what the Hispanic Women say is based on their lived experience.

Questions

1. What has your life been like? Are you satisfied with it? What will you do in the future? What relation is there between what you do every day and God?
2. Who taught you to pray? Which was the first prayer you learned? Who talked to you about God during your childhood? What did they tell you about God?
3. How are you the same or different from your grandparents and parents in religious matters?
4. What do you think about God? How would you describe or draw God? What do you think about Jesus? About Mary? Who are your favorite saints? Do they take care of you?

5. In difficult moments, to whom do you pray? Has your religion helped you in those moments? Have you ever doubted your faith?
6. What is the best thing that you have done or that has happened to you? What is the worst thing that you have done or that has happened to you?
7. Do you read the Bible? Why? Which is your favorite story? Which one do you like the least or have difficulties with?

Apéndice

Estas son las preguntas que se utilizaron en las reuniones que se llevaron a cabo para recoger el material en el que este libro está basado. Las preguntas no fueron invención de las autoras sino que nacieron de los muchos años que ellas llevan escuchando atentamente a las Mujeres Hispanas que como ellas luchan por su liberación.

1. Cuéntanos de tu vida. ¿Estás satisfecha contigo misma? ¿Qué vas a hacer en el futuro? ¿Qué relación hay entre lo que tú haces todos los días y Dios?
2. ¿Quién te enseñó a rezar? ¿Cuál fue la primera oración que aprendiste? ¿Quién te habló de Dios cuando eras pequeña? ¿Qué te decían de Dios?
3. ¿En qué te pareces y en qué eres diferente a tus abuelitas y abuelitos y a tu mamá y papá en cuanto a cosas de religión?
4. ¿Cómo te imaginas a Dios? ¿Cómo describirías o pintarías a Dios? ¿Qué piensas de Jesús? ¿Y de María? ¿Quiénes son tus santos favoritos?
5. En momentos difíciles, ¿a quién le rezas? En esos momentos, ¿te ha ayudado tu religión? ¿Has dudado de la fe en algún momento?
6. ¿Qué es lo mejor que has hecho o que te ha pasado en toda tu vida? ¿Qué es lo peor que has hecho o que te ha pasado en toda tu vida?
7. ¿Lees la Biblia? ¿Por qué? ¿Cuál es tu cuento favorito? ¿Cuál es el cuento que menos te gusta o con el que tienes mayor dificultad?

NOTES

Prologue

1. In the last chapter of this paper we will explain that Hispanic Women as a community of struggle are the theologians. People like ourselves, the authors of this book, are "theological technicians," people with a certain expertise that is validated when it is placed at the service of the theologizing community.
2. This phrase "moods and motivations," will appear from time to time throughout this work. It is part of the definition of religion used by Clifford Geertz. See below, p. 54 and chap. 3, n. 5.
3. Multilayered oppression is discussed by Rosemary Radford Ruether, "A Feminist Perspective," in *Doing Theology in a Divided World*, ed. Virginia Fabella and Sergio Torres (Maryknoll: Orbis Books, 1985), p. 70.
4. Ibid., p. 72.
5. This is not the place to do an analysis of how dualism and hierarchy are intrinsic elements of patriarchy. Suffice it to say that dualism leads to false dichotomies and destructive competition as well as to a false understanding of "different" necessarily implying "better" or "worse." Hierarchy, using dualistic understandings, insists on interpreting "power" as control and domination and, therefore, militates against a true sense of community.
6. Anthony J. Tambasco, "A Critical Appraisal of Segundo's Biblical Hermeneutics," in *The Use of Scripture in Moral Theology*, ed. Charles E. Curran and Richard A. McCormick, S.J. (New York: Paulist Press, 1984), p. 324.
7. Beverly Harrison, *Making The Connections* (Boston: Beacon Press, 1985), p. 250; George Casalis, *Las buenas ideas no caen del cielo* (San José, Costa Rica: Editorial Universitaria Centroamericana, 1979), p. 9, our translation; James Cone, *A Black Theology of Liberation* (New York: Lippincott, 1970), p. 45.
8. There are two reasons for not using the regular word employed by English Bibles, *kingdom*. First, it is obviously a sexist word that presumes that God is male. Second, the concept of kingdom in our world today is both hierarchical and elitist—which is also why we do not use *reign*. The word *kin-dom* makes it clearer that when the fullness of God becomes a day-to-day reality in the world at large, we will all be sisters and brothers—kin to each other.

Chapter 1

1. José Miguez Bonino, *Doing Theology in a Revolutionary Situation* (Philadelphia: Fortress Press, 1975), p. 72.

2. Denis E. Collins, *Paulo Freire: His Life, Works, and Thought* (New York: Paulist Press, 1977), p. 49; J. J. Mueller, *What Are They Saying About Theological Method?* (New York: Paulist Press, 1984), p. 66.
3. Miguez Bonino, *Doing Theology*, p. 72. Please notice that we do not deny ideas or orthodoxy. We are just indicating that the concern for us is in the realm of praxis.
4. Robert J. Schreiter, *Constructing Local Theologies* (Maryknoll: Orbis Books, 1985), pp. 87–88.
5. Aloysius Pieris, "The Place of Non-Christian Religions and Cultures in the Evolution of Third World Theology," in *Irruption of the Third World*, ed. Virginia Fabella and Sergio Torres (Maryknoll: Orbis Books, 1983), pp. 133–37.
6. Juan Carlos Scannone, "Teología cultural popular y discernimiento," in *Cultura popular y filosofía de la liberación* (Buenos Aires, Argentina: Fernando Garcia Cambeiro, 1975), pp. 253–54. All the quotations from this article are our own translations.
7. We refuse to use *minority* or *marginalized* since these labels communicate the way the dominant group sees us. The biblical concept of the remnant seems to describe us better: a hermeneutically privileged group with a significant contribution to make. The function of the remnant in the Bible was to challenge the structures. This is in keeping with the way we understand our task as Hispanic Women: we do not want to participate in present oppressive systems, but rather we want to change those systems.
8. Margaret Farley, "Moral Imperatives for the Ordination of Women," in *Women and Catholic Priesthood: An Expanded Vision*, ed. Anne Marie Gardiner (New York: Paulist Press, 1976), pp. 40–41.
9. On relationship as a basis for full humanity, see Isabel Carter Heyward, *The Redemption of God* (Washington, D.C.: University Press of America, 1982), pp. 1–18. For amplification on the need to understand the political aspect of relationships, see Janice Raymond, "Female Friendship and Feminist Ethics," in *Women's Consciousness, Women's Conscience*, ed. Barbara Hilkert Andolson, Christine E. Gudorf, and Mary D. Pellauer (San Francisco: Harper & Row, 1985), pp. 161–74.
10. This concept of *La Raza* is not a new one. For decades October 12 has been celebrated as "*La Raza* Day" throughout Latin America and among Hispanics in the United States. Virgilio Elizondo makes extensive use of this concept. See Virgilio Elizondo, *Galilean Journey—The Mexican-American Promise* (Maryknoll: Orbis Books, 1983), pp. 5–18.
11. Scannone sees these two lines, the cultural-popular religiosity one and the economic-political one, as two different lines being followed in Latin America. We believe that the bringing together of these two lines is most important for Hispanic Women's Liberation Theology.
12. Mary Elizabeth Hunt, "Feminist Liberation Theology: The Development of Method in Construction" (Ph.D. dissertation, Graduate Theological Union, 1980), p. 161.
13. Gustavo Gutiérrez, *A Theology of Liberation* (Maryknoll: Orbis Books, 1973), pp. 36, 30.
14. Elizondo, *Galilean Journey*, p. 24.
15. Ibid., pp. 16–18.
16. Gutiérrez, *Theology of Liberation*, pp. 13, 3.

17. Antonio Gramsci, *Prison Notebook*, ed. and trans. Quintin Hoare and Geoffrey Nowell Smith (New York: International Publishers, 1975), pp. 6, 330.

18. Ibid., p. 9.

19. Ibid.

Chapter 2

1. The belief among the people is that Mary, the Mother of Jesus, appeared in Mexico with certain human features and dress; the title she is given there is Our Lady of Guadalupe. It is under this title that Mary was declared by the Catholic church "Patroness of the Americas." Mary also appeared in Santo Domingo but with different features and dress from the way she appeared in Mexico; there she is called Our Lady of Altagracia. Though the official church teaching is that it is the same person who appeared in both places, this is not at all clear in the minds of the people, who most often seem to think that each of the titles under which Mary is honored is in reality a different person. Nothing illustrates this better than the following story. During one of the processions in which the statue of Our Lady of San Juan de Los Lagos (another title given to Mary originating in northern Mexico—there is great devotion to Mary under this title among Mexican Americans, especially those who live in Texas) was being carried by a group of men, one of them stumbled. The statue tilted and was in danger of falling. One of the women participating in the procession, noticing the danger at hand, shouted, "Lupita (the nickname of Our Lady of Guadalupe), help Juanita (the nickname of Our Lady of San Juan de Los Lagos)"—as if Lupita and Juanita were not one and the same person.

2. Olga had shown us a holy card (picture) of "the saint" to which Adela refers here. It was the picture of Jesus on the cross. For these women, obviously, this "saint" was not divine and was not the same person as the Jesus of the Gospels.

3. "Ejaculations" is the name given to very short prayers addressed to different saints and/or God. The are a sort of mantra. There used to be the custom of saying many of them because the church taught/teaches that one can gain indulgences for saying ejaculations. Indulgences are given for a specific number of days or years, and they are applied to the temporal punishment that one suffers in purgatory for sins even if they have been forgiven by the priest in confession.

4. On Ash Wednesday, the day that initiates Lent, it is the custom for Roman Catholics to receive ashes. Either the priest or some other appointed person puts ashes on the forehead in the form of a cross. Up to recently the words used while the ashes were being placed on the forehead were: "Remember, man, that thou are dust and to dust thou shall return." More recently they use some formula inviting the person to repentance and conversion.

5. The words of the song give a clear picture of Lupe's theology in reference to her work and her life. The song talks about the abiding presence of God as a source of courage. It repeatedly encourages the Christian to risk whatever is needed in order to be a true witness of the faith. The song finishes by exalting those who are poor and oppressed and promising them the Kingdom of God precisely because they are despised by the powerful.

6. Spiritism is often mistakenly associated with popular religiosity. Spiritism has to do with divination, to which only a few elected ones have access. The religious understandings and practices of popular religiosity are available to all and influence a much larger segment of the Hispanic community than spiritism does. Notice that though María abhors spiritism, her extensive devotion to saints is one of the main elements of popular religiosity.

7. This phrase, "Catholic by birth," is very common among Hispanics. It clearly indicates that the roots in Catholicism go beyond the practice of her faith at that time—things like praying every day, going to confession and communion, etc.

8. At the beginning of this long part of María's sharing, she did not ascribe to God either gender nor make it clear whether God for her was a thing or a person. Direct and indirect object pronouns make this possible in Spanish. In translating we used God here because, to use an article in English, we would have had to define both gender and whether we are referring to a person or a thing. As María went on, she eventually defined God as male. It was quite clear that she has amalgamated "Jesus" and "God" and that she did not care to make too clear whether she was referring to one or the other. It was also quite clear that God is both personal and impersonal for María. God is the father and mother she did not have when she was a child; but God also is a force.

9. The discussion went on but we were not able to explain adequately to Olivia the incongruence we felt existed between her examples and the gender she associates with God.

Chapter 3

1. The term *anthropological poverty* is found in "Doing Theology in a Divided World: Final Statement of the Sixth EATWOT Conference," in *Doing Theology in a Divided World*, ed. Fabella and Torres, p. 185. Paul Tillich discusses being and not being in *Systematic Theology* (Chicago: University of Chicago Press, 1951), vol. 1, p. 14. Cultural survival is discussed by Schreiter in *Constructing Local Theologies*, p. 44.

2. Nancy Hartsock, "Feminist Theory and the Development of Revolutionary Strategy," in *Capitalist Patriarchy and the Case for Socialist Feminism*, ed. Zillah R. Eisenstein (New York: Monthly Review Press, 1979), pp. 59, 61.

3. Gutiérrez, *Theology of Liberation*, p. 10.

4. Hartsock, "Feminist Theory," p. 68.

5. Tillich, pp. 35, 38, 40.

6. Quotes are from Gutiérrez, *Theology of Liberation*, p. 11. The idea of a hermeneutic of suspicion is found in Juan Luis Segundo, *The Liberation of Theology* (Maryknoll: Orbis Books, 1982), pp. 7–38.

7. Elisabeth Schüssler Fiorenza, *In Memory of Her* (New York: Crossroad, 1983), pp. 29, 30, 32.

8. Gutiérrez, *Theology of Liberation*, p. 13.

9. Clifford Geertz, *The Interpretation of Culture* (New York: Basic Books, 1973), p. 90.

10. We use "official" with quotation marks because great variations exist in the Roman Catholic tradition, especially when it comes to practices. Official written

Roman Catholic theology holds both the Bible and tradition as equally central. But in Latin America and among Hispanics in the United States, what goes on inside the church buildings and is organized and often led by priests revolves much more around tradition than around the Bible—and the tradition includes other than Christian understandings, as we go on to explain in the text.

11. Pieris, "Place of Non-Christian Religions," in *Irruption*, ed. Fabella and Torres, p. 134.

12. The definition of enculturation is found in Paulo Agirrebaltzategi, *Configuración eclesial de las culturas* (Bilbao, Spain: Universidad de Deusto, 1976), p. 82. This is our own translation. The author explains the three terms *acculturation*, *enculturation*, and *culturization* on pp. 81–82. He uses the latter one to indicate that what has become cultural expression is what is "transcultural or transcendent. It also means the form in which culturally the Gospel message is realized in the Church." We use the term here in a narrower sense to mean simply that which has become a cultural expression.

13. For example, notice María's rejection of spiritism above, pp. 32–38.

14. On "prescribed beliefs and norms," see Schreiter, *Constructing Local Theologies*, p. 125. On emphasizing church tradition, see Segundo, *Liberation of Theology*, p. 185.

15. The same is often true of sermons we hear on Sundays. It is not considered "good theology" when Hispanic Women do it, but it is all right when the priests do it.

16. Schreiter, *Constructing Local Theologies*, p. 125.

17. Geertz, *Interpretation of Culture*, p. 90.

18. Juan J. Sosa, "Religiosidad popular y sincretismo religioso: Santería y espiritismo," *Documentaciones Sureste*, no. 4 (March 1983), p. 18.

19. Ibid., pp. 14–26.

20. Tom. F. Driver, *Christ in a Changing World* (New York: Crossroad, 1981), pp. 32–81.

21. Because this statement says what many know but are afraid to verbalize, we think that the reader needs to remember the commitment to orthopraxis of Hispanic Women's Liberation Theology and its insistence on the lived experience of Hispanic Women as its source. The importance Hispanic Women give to Jesus seems to be in direct proportion to whether or not they participate in church movements and organizations. The Hispanic Women whose Christianity is simply part of their culture know very little about Jesus and do not pray to him. This is noticeable even in the small number of Hispanic Women who are quoted in this book.

Hispanic Women's Liberation Theology will necessarily have to develop its own Christology for several reasons: (a) Christology is part of Western Christianity, which acts as paradigm for the "Christianity" of Hispanic Women; (b) the renewal that has taken place in the Roman Catholic church since the Second Vatican Council in the 1960s includes a serious effort to make Scripture much more central than it has been before. This has led to such movements as the "Cursillo" and "Charismatics" in which Hispanic Women are involved and which use the Bible extensively; (c) Hispanic Women who attend other than Roman Catholic churches do know the Bible and use it.

22. Compare the difference in interpretation and explanation of Guadalupe between Elizondo and Lafaye. See Virgilio Elizondo, *La morenita* (Liguori, MO: Liguori

Publications, 1981), and J. Lafaye, *Quetzalcoatl et Guadalupe* (Paris: Gallimard, 1974).

23. Geertz, *Interpretation of Culture*, p. 90.

24. We wish to thank Professor Tom F. Drriver who read an earlier version of this section and offered helpful comments.

25. According to Niebuhr, in this model the people "feel no great tension between church and world, the social laws and the Gospel, the workings of divine grace and human effort, the ethics of salvation and the ethics of social conservation or progress. On the one hand they interpret culture through Christ, regarding those elements in it as most important which are most accordant with his work and person; on the other hand they understand Christ through culture, selecting from his teaching and action as well as from the Christian doctrine about him such points as seem to agree with what is best in civilization." H. Richard Niebuhr, *Christ and Culture* (New York: Harper & Row, 1951), p. 83.

26. Ibid., p. xi.

27. Agirrebaltzategi, *Configuración eclesial*, p. 364. See also Segundo, *Liberation of Theology*, pp. 185-86.

28. Agirrebaltzategi, p. 62. Definition of culture comes from Mary Lou Dehavenon, "Cultural Anthropology and the Values of Community, Diversity, Poverty, Femininity, Peace, and Change in the United States in 1984" (Lecture delivered at the Leadership Conference of Women Religious, Kansas City, MO, August 1984).

29. Agirrebaltzategi, *Configuración eclesial*, pp. 65, 66. By his concept of "organic structure," we did not understand Agirrebaltzategi to indicate or suggest culture as destiny; if he did, we would not agree with him.

30. Ibid., pp. 66-67.

31. Julio D. De Zan, "Para una filosofía de la cultura y una filosofía política nacional," in *Cultura popular y filosofía de la liberación* (Buenos Aires: Fernando Garcia Cambeiro, 1975), pp. 89-90. Since we translated this from the Spanish, we chose to use the feminine pronouns in English when Spanish uses pronouns that are not gender specific.

32. For the idea of culture within culture, see James W. Green, *Cultural Awareness in the Human Service* (New York: Prentice-Hall, 1982), p. 7. On culture as a way of comprehending and valuing self, others, and nature, see De Zan, *Filosofía*, p. 100.

33. Ibid.

34. Ibid., p. 89. In our use of De Zan, we have left out the phrase "historically determined" because we do not believe in determinism of any kind. We would accept, however, "historically conditioned."

35. To some, our claim that Hispanic Women's culture is being birthed might sound like an exaggeration. We would simply ask them to come and participate in an "Hispanas Unidas Conference" in San Antonio, or in one of the gatherings of "Hispanic Women of the South Bronx." It will be very obvious that new patterns of behavior, relationality, and understandings are emerging.

Chapter 4

1. Judith Vaughan, *Sociality, Ethics, and Social Change* (Boston: University Press of America, 1983), p. 197.

2. Peter J. Paris, "The Task of Religious Social Ethics in the Light of Black Theology," in *Liberation and Ethics*, ed. Charles Amjad-Ali and W. Alvin Pitcher (Chicago: Center for The Scientific Study of Religion, 1985), pp. 140–42. We are using Paris's proposal for an adequate religious social ethics as the framework for our discussion here.

3. See above, chap. 1, n. 9.

4. Vaughan, pp. 197–98.

5. Paris, p. 141.

6. Dorothy Emmet, *The Moral Prism* (New York: St. Martin's Press, 1979), p. 7.

7. Ibid., p. 10.

8. Ibid., p. 11.

9. Ibid., pp. 12–13. We are not advocating here a situation ethics theory that takes into account only one single feature of the situation at hand without relating it to other features or principles. See Emmet, p. 159, n. 3.

10. In 1982 the Archdiocese of New York published the results of a survey that was done among Hispanics. To the statement posed by the interview, "Abortion is always wrong," the study indicated that "64.4% of the Latinos believed firmly that abortion is always wrong . . . ." (vol. 1, p. 38). However, using the 1980 statistics of the Department of Health of the City of New York, the study indicates that "for the year 1980 abortions among Puerto Ricans exceeded births by 50%. . . . In hypothetical terms, of 5 pregnant Puerto Rican women in the year 1980 in New York City, 3 would have an abortion. . . ." (vol. 2, p. 183). Office of Pastoral Research, Archdiocese of New York, *Hispanics in New York: Religious, Cultural, and Social Experiences*, 2 vols. (Archdiocese of New York, 1980).

Chapter 5

1. The definition of dialogue comes from Paulo Freire, *Cultural Action for Freedom* (Cambridge: Harvard Educational Review, 1970), p. 45. Some use the word *animator* to refer to what we call the *enabler*. In Spanish we would use the word *animadora* since that is the best translation of *enabler*. For discussion of the enabler, see Frei Betto, quoted in Segundo, *Liberation of Theology*, p. 239. For discussion of dishonesty in the dialogue see Freire, *Cultural Action*, p. 52.

2. Paulo Freire, "Education, Liberation and the Church," *Religious Education* 79 (Fall 1984): 527–28.

3. This process or variations of it has been used widely by different women's groups to develop strategies or as a process of conscientization. We are not interested in claiming that our process is unique or different. Our interest is only to explain the process we use.

4. Lecture by Gloria Durka, Union Theological Seminary, New York, November 1984.

5. On liturgy as announcing the future and denouncing the present, see Freire, *Cultural Action*, p. 21. Gloria Durka gives three reasons for the importance of freeing the religious imagination:
    1. Religious imagination enables us to find depth in the ordinary—enables us to see that the ordinary has significance.

2. It helps us to live in truth by bridging the gap between matter and spirit, overcoming dualism.

3. Religious imagination helps us to live with a sense of possibility—possibility to create a new world order.

(Lecture given at Union Theological Seminary, New York, November 1984.)

6. Gutiérrez, *Theology of Liberation*, pp. 36–37.

7. This sense of the divine is very, very often expressed by Hispanic Women. We have often heard it at home from our mothers and grandmothers.

8. Sebastian Kappen, "Orientations for an Asian Theology," in *Asia's Struggle for Humanity*, ed. Virginia Fabella (Maryknoll: Orbis Books, 1980), p. 118.

9. Carlos H. Abesamis, "Faith and Life Reflections from the Grassroots in the Philippines," in *Asia's Struggle*, ed. Fabella, p. 137. Theological technicians likewise need competence in process design and group process facilitation. Because they are part of the community, theological technicians are "real theologians."

10. William B. Kennedy, "Conversation with Paulo Freire," in *Religious Education* 79 (Fall 1984): 520.

11. Ibid. Freire says, "The conditions, the political awareness, the social situation, the material conditions in which we are, all have to do with the reading of a book. The question is that the language is not in itself so difficult. What is more difficult sometimes to understand is the dialectical way of life. How is it possible, for example, for one to grasp reality which is moving unless with a language which also moves? That is, if you don't use a formal way of writing, it is difficult with those who have a formal way of thinking. Nevertheless, I think it does not mean that I could not write much more simply. After that first book I think that the other ones are much more simple."

12. We are grateful to Professor William B. Kennedy for the suggestions he gave us regarding some of these criteria.

13. We are here disagreeing with Gustavo Gutiérrez. See Gutiérrez, "Reflections From a Latin American Perspective: Finding Our Way to Talk About God," in *Irruption*, ed. Fabella and Torres, pp. 224–25.

14. See Abesamis, *Faith and Life Reflections*, p. 137. This phrase was used by John Paul II during his trip to Mexico in 1979. He said that the church should be "voice of the voiceless." It is to his credit that he did not credit the church as already fulfilling this task!

15. David Tracy, *Blessed Rage for Order* (New York: Seabury Press, 1978), p. 71.

16. This is an adaptation of Tracy's "criteria of appropriateness," which has to do with "appropriate understandings of the Christian understanding of existence" (Tracy, p. 72). Hispanic Women's Liberation Theology has to modify his definition of appropriateness because Hispanic Women's experience has not been taken into consideration when the Christian understanding of existence has been defined.

17. We were pleasantly surprised to see that Abesamis and Kappen suggest very similar "criteria of appropriateness" to the one we present here. Abesamis, *Faith and Life Reflections*, pp. 123–39; Kappen, "Asian Theology," pp. 108–22.

DATE DUE

12-21-90	"RESERVE"		
5-30-91	MAR - - 2001		
OCT 2 3 1991			
NOV 07 199	APR 0 9 2002 DEC 0 2 2002		
FEB 05 1992	JAN - 7 2004		
FEB 2 2 1992	APR 7 2004		
FEB 2 3 1993	6-2005		
MAR 3 0 1993	MAR 0 4 2007		
MAR 3 1 1994	JUN 0 2 2013		
8-3-94			
MAR 2 0 1995			
APR 0 1 1997			
07/14/99			
MAR 2 9 2000			
"RESERVE"			
MAR - - 2000			

GAYLORD   PRINTED IN U.S.A.